Prayer

For Beginners

About Richard Webster

Author of over seventy-five books, Richard Webster is one of New Zealand's most prolific writers. His best-selling books include *Spirit Guides & Angel Guardians*, *Creative Visualization for Beginners*, *Soul Mates*, *Is Your Pet Psychic?*, *Practical Guide to Past-Life Memories*, *Astral Travel for Beginners*, *Miracles*, and the four-book series on archangels: *Michael*, *Gabriel*, *Raphael*, and *Uriel*.

A noted psychic, Richard is a member of the National Guild of Hypnotherapists (USA), the Association of Professional Hypnotherapists and Parapsychologists (UK), the International Registry of Professional Hypnotherapists (Canada), and the Psychotherapy and Hypnotherapy Institute of New Zealand. When not touring, he resides in New Zealand with his wife and family.

To Write to the Author

If you wish to contact the author or would like more information about this book, please write to the author in care of Llewellyn Worldwide and we will forward your request. Both the author and publisher appreciate hearing from you and learning of your enjoyment of this book and how it has helped you. Llewellyn Worldwide cannot guarantee that every letter written to the author can be answered, but all will be forwarded. Please write to:

Richard Webster
℅ Llewellyn Worldwide
2143 Wooddale Drive, Dept. 978-0-7387-1538-4
Woodbury, MN 55125-2989, U.S.A.

Please enclose a self-addressed stamped envelope for reply,
or $1.00 to cover costs. If outside the U.S.A., enclose
an international postal reply coupon.

Many of Llewellyn's authors have websites with additional information and resources. For more information, please visit our website at http://www.llewellyn.com.

Richard Webster

Prayer

For Beginners

Discovering the Language
of Your Soul

Llewellyn Publications
Woodbury, Minnesota

First Edition
First Printing, 2009

Book design by Steffani Sawyer
Cover art © 2009 by Michael Hitoshi/Digital Vision/PunchStock
Cover design by Lisa Novak
Editing by Brett Fechheimer
Llewellyn is a registered trademark of Llewellyn Worldwide, Ltd.

Library of Congress Cataloging-in-Publication Data
Webster, Richard, 1946–
  Prayer for beginners : discovering the language of your soul /
Richard Webster.—1st ed.
      p.   cm.
  Includes bibliographical references and index.
  ISBN 978-0-7387-1538-4
  1. Prayer. I. Title.
  BL560.W44 2009
  204'.3—dc22
                                                    2009011832

Llewellyn Publications
A Division of Llewellyn Worldwide, Ltd.
2143 Wooddale Drive, Dept. 978-0-7387-1538-4
Woodbury, Minnesota 55125-2989, U.S.A.
www.llewellyn.com

Printed in the United States of America

For my granddaughter
Kiera Grace Martin

contents

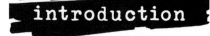
introduction

Where is that secret place—dost thou ask, "Where?"
O soul, it is the secret place of prayer!
—ALFRED, LORD TENNYSON

A few months ago, a friend asked if he could borrow a book. I took him into my library, and while looking for the book he wanted, I found something else that I thought might interest him.

"Oh God!" he exclaimed. "That's the book I've been looking for."

It was only afterward that I thought about his choice of words. My friend is an atheist, yet he used the words "Oh God!" Even though he'd deny it, in a sense he was giving God a prayer of thanks for helping him locate the book he was searching for. This made me think that we all pray at certain times in our lives. Whenever we need help or guidance, we look to the divine.

Isn't it fascinating that most people want a closer connection to God, yet so few people make prayer a regular part of their lives? There are many reasons for this. Most people lead busy lives, and once work and family responsibilities have been met, there is little time for anything else. Other people choose not to pray, as it seems better to keep God at a distance. Praying may seem too hard. After all, it requires a degree of discipline and commitment. But the biggest problem in my experience is that most people don't know how to pray.

I have thought about writing a book on this subject for many years, but my own fears and doubts held me back. After all, I haven't spent years studying religion at a university level. I can't claim a special relationship with God. I sometimes doubt that God exists. Yet I'm aware of a spiritual dimension in my life, and over the years I have helped many people develop a closer relationship with God. A number of people have encouraged me to write this book, and after putting it off for as long as I could, I finally decided to write it. I hope this book will help you establish and enjoy a closer connection with the divine, too.

I also hope this book will be useful to you, no matter which religion or tradition you belong to, and even if you have no religion at all. Many people today are finding their own way to God.

As a child, I believed God was a powerful old man with a long white beard who sat on a cloud and saw everything that happened on earth. I never found this image comforting. In fact, it was alarming to think God was watching my every thought and deed. Of course, none of us have any idea what God looks like.

An unknown fourteenth-century English monk wrote a spiritual tract called *The Cloud of Unknowing*. He wrote: "But now you will ask me, 'How am I to think of God himself, and what is He?' and I cannot answer you except to say 'I do not know!' For with this question you have brought me into the cloud of unknowing. Of God Himself can no man think."[1]

Dictionaries say God is a supreme being, a deity. Different religions call God by different names, such as Allah, Brahman, Yahweh, Krishna, and Buddha. God is sometimes called the absolute, the universal life force, the divine, the Goddess, the source of life, the Tao, the Ultimate, the Great Spirit, or Great Mystery.

Throughout the ages, many people have tried to define God. St. Augustine (354–430) described God as "That Which Is." St. Anselm (1033–1109), at one

---

1. Clifton Wolters, trans., *The Cloud of Unknowing* (Baltimore, MD: Penguin Books, 1961), 5.

time Archbishop of Canterbury, wrote, "God is that, the greater than which cannot be conceived." St. Catherine of Siena (1347–80) considered God to be "pure love." St. Teresa of Avila (1515–82) considered God to be "His Majesty" and "Supplier of True Life." Albert Einstein (1879–1955) thought God was the "organizing principle of the universe." Marianne Williamson defines God as "the pure and all-powerful love that rules the universe and lies within us all."[2]

I believe that we are all God. Everything in the universe is God, and we are an integral part of the whole. As we're all part of the universal consciousness, effectively we're God searching for ourselves.

I've been told that it's egotistical to say, "I am God." However, this can't be the case if we're all God.

God is beyond human words or understanding, but can be approached in worship and prayer.

People have used prayer as a way of communicating with God for thousands of years. It has been hypothesized that the first people to pray were Neanderthals who lived between 200,000 and 30,000 BCE.[3] Prayer possibly began as a form of magic, with the magician or shaman calling down power from the heavens. The ancient Assyrians and Babylonians

---

2. Marianne Williamson, foreword in Richard Carlson, PhD, and Benjamin Shield, *For the Love of God: Handbook for the Spirit* (Novato, CA: New World Library, 1999), xv–xvi.

3. Philip Zaleski and Carol Zaleski, *Prayer: A History* (Boston: Houghton Mifflin, 2005), 15–17.

were praying five thousand years ago, and records of prayers to the moon goddess Sin and to a god named Tammuz have been discovered. A prayer of gratitude for success in battle was sent to the Babylonian sun god Marduk. This dates back to about 1200 BCE.

Many ancient Egyptian prayers still survive, as they were engraved on the backs of scarabs and written on sheets of papyrus. They are largely prayers of praise and requests for protection for family and loved ones. Some were incantations that were used in protection magic. The Egyptian Book of the Dead consists largely of magical incantations and prayers that were used to protect the deceased in the next world.

An ancient Egyptian prayer inscribed on a scarab and placed with the heart of a mummified corpse may be the oldest prayer in existence. Sir E. A. Wallis Budge translated it:

> *Heart of my mother! Heart of my mother! Heart of my being! Oppose me not in my evidence [or testimony]. Thrust me not aside before the Judges [of the dead]. Fall not away from me before the Guardian of the Balance [who weighs the soul against a feather]. Thou art my KA in my body [KA was originally the divine spiritual aspect of the human body that survives death], Khnemu making sound my members. Come thou forth to the place of happiness [or felicity] whither we would go. Make not my name to stink with the Assessors, who make men, during*

> *my existence. Make good a good bearing with*
> *joy of heart at the weighing of words and deeds.*
> *Utter no falsehood concerning me in the pres-*
> *ence of the Great God.*[4]

The ancient Greeks practiced a form of poetic prayer, which began with an invocation to the gods. The ritual began with hand washing, followed by the prayer, a sacrifice, and food and drink. Prayers were frequently transformed into hymns to the gods. Homer (c. eighth century BCE) included the prayer of Diomedes to the goddess Athena in his epic poem *The Iliad*.

The Romans began their prayers with an invocation to the deity concerned. Their prayers included requests and praise. Their most important prayers were *votum* (which means "vow"). The person asked the god for a specific favor, and promised something in return. This could be a sacrifice for a small request, or the building of a temple for something of major importance.

The 150 Psalms of David in the Bible are the best-known prayers in Judaism. Jewish people pray two or three times a day, as well as saying a benediction before meals. Early Christians also said their prayers three times a day, when they recited the Lord's Prayer. They also prayed before eating.

---

4. E. A. Wallis Budge, *Amulets and Superstitions* (London: Oxford University Press, 1930), 139–40. Reprinted by Dover Publications, New York, 1978.

The first known Christian document that taught people how to pray was written by Quintus Septimius Florens Tertullianus (c.160–c.220). Tertullian, as he is usually known, was the son of a Roman centurion. After becoming a Christian he became concerned with the worldliness inside the Church, and criticized Pope Callistus for forgiving adultery and fornication. He wrote many books and treatises, including *On Prayer*. In this text he outlined the Christian faith using an in-depth analysis of the Lord's Prayer, which he called the epitome of the entire Gospel.

Tertullian also included a great deal of advice on how and when to pray. For instance, he recommended praying at 9:00 AM, noon, and 3:00 PM, as well as first thing in the morning, and in the evening. He also suggested people pray before eating, and even before having a bath.

Origen (c.185–254) was the first Christian father to write on the subject of prayer in Greek. He wrote many books, including *De Oratione* (*On Prayer*). In this book he gave advice on what to pray for, using the Gospels to provide examples. He provided answers to people who think prayer is unnecessary and superfluous. He also, like Tertullian, provided a detailed commentary on the Lord's Prayer. St. Cyprian (c.200–258), another early Christian father, also wrote an important commentary on the Lord's Prayer, and many other authors carried on this tradition with their own commentaries on what is by far the most famous Christian prayer.

Prayer plays an important role in Islam, too. Every devout Muslim faces Mecca five times a day and recites the *salat* ("daily prayer"). On Fridays, the noon prayer is replaced with the *salat al-jumu'ah* ("Friday prayer"). Islamic prayers do not include personal requests, as they are acts of adoration of Allah. Before praying, Muslims purify themselves by performing their ablutions in pure water or, if necessary, in sand.

Hindu prayers involve both meditation and praise to the deity involved. Believers receive remission from their sins if they recite their prayers conscientiously and with a pure heart.

Prayer is also a factor in Taoism and Chinese Buddhism. Prayers, accompanied by a small bell, are said at morning, noon, and night. An important prayer for the dead is recited at funerals, thirty days after the death, the anniversary of the death, and on the deceased's birthday. Monks will also say prayers for people for a small fee. These prayers are known as *tsai-fei*.

This book contains a number of different methods of praying for you to experiment with. You will probably find that you prefer one method to the others. You may like two or three of them. Some methods might seem more effective than others. Once you have decided on the method that is best for you, work on it and develop your skills at this type of prayer. Every now and then, experiment again with some of the other methods. There is no single path to the divine, and you are likely to find that using a variety of methods will increase the effectiveness of your prayers.

one

What Is Prayer?

Prayer helps us contact sources of inspiration
and wisdom that transcend the rational,
analytical side of the mind.
Prayer provides a sense of hope and meaning—
the certainty that we are part of a pattern
that is purposeful and intelligent.
—LARRY DOSSEY

Although my parents were not religious, as a young child I was encouraged to say my prayers before going to sleep. The two prayers I remember were not particularly comforting to me as a small child:

> *Now I lay me down to sleep,*
> *I pray the Lord my soul to keep.*
> *If I should die before I wake,*
> *I pray the Lord my soul to take.*

> *Matthew, Mark, Luke, and John,*
> *Bless the bed that I lay on.*
> *Four angels to my bed,*
> *Four angels 'round my head.*
> *One to watch, and one to pray,*
> *And two to bear my soul away.*

The word *prayer* comes from two related Latin words: *precarius*, which means "obtained by begging," and *precari*, which means "to entreat." According to a Gallup poll, 90 percent of people in the United States pray, and 60 percent of these people consider prayer to play an important part in their everyday lives.[5]

Prayer is the act of communicating with the divine. It enables people to achieve unity with the creator of the universe. Prayer is the language of the soul. It is a conversation with God, the gods, the supernatural, the Creator, the Source, the sacred, the holy, or the transcendent.

This naturally leads to another important question: Is God out there somewhere in heaven, or is God inside you, me, and everyone else? If God is inside your mind, your heart, and every other part of your body, you can transmit God's love and blessings everywhere you go. I believe God is inside everyone.

There's a wonderful old story that illustrates this. A teacher said to a student, "I'll give you an orange if

---

5. Margaret Poloma and George Gallup, *Varieties of Prayer* (Harrisburg, PA: Trinity Press International, 1991), ix.

you can tell me where God is." The student immediately replied, "I'll give you two oranges if you can tell me where God is not!"

At first glance, the idea that God is everywhere is at odds with the first line of the Lord's Prayer: "Our Father, who art in heaven." However, St. Paul talked about "Christ in you" when he wrote: "To whom God would make known what is the riches of the glory of this mystery among the Gentiles; which is Christ in you, the hope of glory" (Colossians 1:27). The first two words of the Lord's Prayer (*Our Father*) clearly show that every person on the planet is related, not only to God but also to everyone else.

Prayer is also a state of being. It comes from the heart as much as the head. A prayer does not necessarily need any words at all; when you are in a state of prayer, you are in communication with the divine, and words are superfluous. This means that a gambler crossing his fingers before tossing the dice may well be in a state of prayer.

Prayer is a universal spiritual language that is available to everyone. People of all traditions and creeds pray. If someone has a problem, a friend might suggest that he or she "pray on it." There are many other popular sayings involving prayer, such as "The family that prays together stays together." One dating from the Second World War is "On a wing and a prayer." This means something has little chance of success. A sadly true saying is "Worry is a prayer for something you don't want." I particularly love the anonymous one-liner "As long as there are tests, there will be prayer in school."

Prayer plays a central role in all religions. According to William James, the great American philosopher, there can be no question of religion without prayer. He wrote that prayer "is the very soul and essence of religion."[6] Prayer is the expression of the deepest feelings of the person to the object of his or her faith.

Prayer, by its very nature, assumes that there is someone or something that created the universe. This being cares about all of humanity and wants to communicate with each and every person. This concept is easier to accept when you realize that every person on this planet is part of God (the Tao, Allah, Brahma, Universal Life Force, or any other name you prefer to use) anyway.

Prayer gives us access to the mystical force behind all creation.

There are different types of prayer. Prayers that are difficult to categorize as a single prayer can include several categories:

Petition

Prayers of petition ask God for a personal request. Prayers of this sort are extremely common, as people

---

6. William James, *The Varieties of Religious Experience* (London: Longmans, Green, 1903), 121.

often pray when they need something. These are usually personal calls for help, and include topics such as asking for an improvement in health, prosperity, success, or longevity. In some ways, these can be considered selfish prayers. However, prayers of petition also include spiritual requests, such as asking God to remain close to the person who is praying. One of the Prophet Muhammad's better known *hadīths* (traditional sayings) is "Nothing is more honorable in God's eyes than petition."

Intercession

Prayers of petition are requests for help for the person making the prayer. Prayers of intercession are made to ask for help for others. People pray for friends and members of their family. They may even pray for people they do not know, requesting help for the sick and weak, and for groups, countries, and even the whole world. When Jesus was on the cross he made an intercessory prayer, asking God to forgive the people who were crucifying him. "Father, forgive them; for they know not what they do" (Luke 23:34).

Praise and Adoration

Prayers of praise are made to thank God for His many blessings, such as food, health, loved ones, and life. Prayers of adoration praise God while acknowledging

His total mystery. Although this is a prayer of submission, many people believe that as we bless God, we become blessed in return.

Gratitude

Prayers of gratitude thank God for the blessings in our lives. Everyone has a great deal to be thankful for, starting with the miracle of life itself. There are times when prayers of gratitude are necessary to thank the divine for a special blessing. Falling in love, the birth of a baby, or a near escape from danger are all times when people want to thank the creator of the universe. The Psalms contain many examples of prayers of gratitude. Here are the first two verses of Psalm 138:

> *I will praise thee with my whole heart: before the gods will I sing praise unto thee. I will worship toward thy holy temple, and praise thy name for thy loving kindness and for thy truth: for thou hast magnified thy word above all thy name.*

Confession

Confession plays an important part in most religions. It occurs when people repent their sins and ask for forgiveness. Buddhist monks publicly confess their sins before Buddha and their congregations. The Catholic Church has the confessional, where sinners can receive penance for their sins. Confessional prayers are made to God, as He alone can grant pardon and peace of mind.

You can confess any thought or deed that you regret. This might include impatience with a colleague or family member, or thinking negative thoughts about someone. You do not need to have committed a major crime to confess your sins.

Mystical Union

Prayers of mystical union are an ecstatic union in which words cease to have any relevance or meaning. It is a union in which God and the person making the prayer become as one. Prayers of this sort are called contemplative prayers.

Thanksgiving

Prayers of thanksgiving thank God for the blessings that we normally take for granted, such as friends, food, and good health. A grace before a meal is a good example of this type of prayer.

Prayers and Psychic Occurrences

There have been many instances in which prayer has opened people up to paranormal experiences, such as telepathy and precognition. On one occasion, while praying, St. Anthony clairvoyantly saw two brothers. One was dead, the other seriously ill. St. Anthony was able to send monks to rescue the dying man.

On many occasions, St. Francis of Assisi involuntarily levitated while saying his prayers. However, his levitation abilities were eclipsed by St. Joseph of Cupertino, who was able to levitate for considerable lengths of time. He was known as the "leaping friar."

In the late 1960s, Dr. Karlis Osis, director of the American Society for Psychical Research, performed a series of informal experiments into religion and parapsychology using small groups of volunteers. He discovered that the participants appeared to share the same visions and were able to communicate telepathically with each other. He also found that group prayer was more effective than a prayer by an individual, because the group dynamic created feelings of openness, love, and meaningfulness. It is possible that the synchronization of their brain waves was a contributing factor, too.

General George S. Patton demanded a group prayer as the U.S. Third Army advanced into Germany in 1944. After days of torrential rain, he asked chaplain James H. O'Neill to publish a prayer for good weather. The chaplain expressed some doubt, and replied: "May I say, General, that it usually isn't a customary thing among men of my profession to pray for clear weather to kill fellow men." "Chaplain," the general said, "are you teaching me theology or are you the chaplain of the Third Army? I want a prayer."[7]

The chaplain prepared a prayer that was distributed to the troops. In less than twenty-four hours, the skies cleared and a week of superb weather followed. General Patton was so thrilled with the chaplain's prayer that he awarded him the Bronze Star.

Christian Prayer

Christians pray to God the Trinity (Father, Son, and Holy Spirit). Christian prayer was originally based on the Lord's Prayer that Jesus taught to his disciples (Matthew 6:9–15 and Luke 11:2–4). Different traditions vary as to the correct posture for praying. Many Christians kneel, but others sit or stand.

The rosary used by the Roman Catholic Church helps people keep track of the exact number of prayers they have said. Reciting prayers takes considerable concentration, and the use of rosaries means the required number of repetitions can be made without conscious thought. The act of handling an object such as a rosary bead while praying also appears to make the prayer more effective. The rosary releases tension and enhances relaxation, which helps open the person up to spiritual insights. St. Dominic popularized the use of rosaries in the twelfth century.

---

7. George S. Patton, Jr. (annotated by Col. Paul D. Hawkins), *War As I Knew It* (Boston: Houghton Mifflin, 1947), 185.

Islamic Prayer

Islam has a set of practices called the Five Pillars of Islam, to which all Muslims adhere. These practices are monotheism, prayer, fasting, charity, and pilgrimage. Of these, prayer has the most direct impact on the life of a Muslim, as every follower has to pray five times a day.[8] These are ritual prayers, known as *salat*. Muslims can also pray with personal needs and desires, known as *du'a*, or supplication. Muslims usually pray in groups, led by a prayer-leader, as they believe God appreciates this more than solitary prayer. Muslims are called to prayer by a *muezzin*, a man with a pleasing voice who summons people to prayer. The *muezzin* stands in the minaret of a mosque, and makes the call to prayer in Arabic.

Muslims pray every day for two main reasons. Daily prayer reminds them that they are God's servants. Daily prayer also has the benefit that each time they pray, God forgives some of their sins. It is dangerous to miss prayers, as Muhammad said that on Judgment Day, when people's good and bad deeds are examined, God will look at prayers first.

Muslims pray five times a day for another reason also. No matter how busy they happen to be,

---

8. The timing of the five daily prayers is listed in the Qur'an. The actual times change every month because of the different seasons. The official times are: *Fajr* (between first light and sunrise), *Zuhr* (just after midday), *'Asr* (late afternoon), *Maghrib* (just after sunset), and *Isha* (any time after dark).

and no matter what is going on in their lives, they are constantly aware that they have recently prayed and will be praying again very soon. Prayer is never far from their minds.

There are several conditions that have to be met before Muslims can pray. It must be a specific time to pray. They must wash their face, hands, and feet with water before praying. This makes them ritually pure. There are many examples in the Bible of washing before praying, and the Lord gave Moses instruction in this (Exodus 30:17–21). Muslims must pray in clean clothes, and these clothes must cover the body. Consequently, men must pray in long trousers, rather than shorts, and women must cover their hair with a scarf or veil. Prayer must be conducted in a clean environment. They must face Mecca. They must also have the correct mindset to pray effectively. The Qur'an says, "Woe to those that pray and are heedless of their prayers, to those who make display and refuse charity" (Sura 107:1–7).

Muslims perform a sequence of movements while reciting memorized prayers. This enables them to humble themselves before God, and achieve the desired meditative state that allows them to focus entirely on God.

Jewish Prayer

When Jews pray, they enter into a special space that connects them with everyone else who is praying at the same time, or has prayed in the past. This interconnectedness helps them gain a closer connection with God. One of the most important aspects of Jewish prayer is the *kavvanah*, or intention behind the prayer. Some Jews often sway or rock while praying. This is called *shuckling*, and enables them to pray with their entire bodies.

Jewish people enjoy praying in groups, and synagogues provide three services a day to encourage this. Private prayer also plays an important part in Judaism. The three daily services are all related to one of the religion's patriarchs. *Shaharit*, or morning prayer, comes from Abraham, who "got up early in the morning to the place where he stood before the Lord" (Genesis 19:27). *Minhah*, or afternoon prayer, comes from Isaac, who "went out to meditate in the field at the eventide" (Genesis 24:63). *Ma'ariv*, or evening prayer, comes from Jacob. All of these also relate to David the Psalmist, who wrote: "Evening, and morning, and at noon, will I pray, and cry aloud: and he shall hear my voice" (Psalm 55:17).

Jews honor their dead by reciting a prayer called the *Kaddish*. Every service concludes with the Kaddish, and people who are mourning the death of someone participate. A good Jewish son would recite the Kaddish for his deceased parent, every morning and night for eleven months after he or she died. Jews believe that even the worst of sinners spend a maximum of twelve months in hell. As no son can believe his mother or father would ever receive the maximum penalty, the Kaddish is recited for eleven months. The Kaddish provides redemption for the sins of the deceased.

The Kaddish began as a story, which gradually turned into a legend. Apparently, Rabbi Akiba, a renowned second-century scholar, dreamed one night of a sad-looking man who was carrying a large load of wood. He asked the man why he was carrying such a huge load. The man replied that he was actually dead, and was forced to endure the fires of hell for his sins. To make the punishment even more severe, he was also collecting the necessary wood to feed the flames. This poor sinner told Rabbi Akiba that he had a son, but he had failed to teach him anything of the Jewish faith. Would it be possible for the rabbi to find his son and teach him a single Hebrew prayer? If he could, that would put out the fires of hell.

When he woke up, Rabbi Akiba immediately began searching for the man's son. He found him and taught him the Kaddish, the Jewish prayer of sanctification. That night, the rabbi had another dream in which the man reappeared. He wanted to express his gratitude to the rabbi, because when his son recited the Kaddish, all his sins were forgiven and his soul was saved.

A unique factor in Jewish prayer is the presence of prayer shawls and head coverings. The *tallith*, or prayer shawl, is usually made from white wool and has purple or black stripes crossing it. It also usually contains tassels or fringes on the four corners. The top of the shawl is marked with silver or gold thread. Conservative and Orthodox Jews wear the tallith during both private and public prayer.

The *yarmulke*, or skull cap, is worn by most Orthodox Jews. Conservative Jews cover their heads only while they are worshipping. Head coverings are optional at Reform services.

During weekday morning services, male Jews wear the *tefillin*, which are two small leather boxes that contain four passages from the Bible (Deuteronomy 6:4–9, Deuteronomy 11:13–20, Exodus 13:1–10, and Exodus 13:11–16). These are strapped to the arm and forehead. The tefillin are not worn on the Sabbath or during festivals. They are also not worn by men from the time they hear of a relative's death until after that person's funeral.

Buddhist Prayer

Buddhists seek enlightenment so they can help all living things. They believe in reincarnation, and are committed to a path that extends well beyond this one lifetime. They are helped in this by observing the Three Jewels of Buddhism: Buddha himself,

Dharma (Buddha's teachings), and *Sangha* (the monks and other spiritual teachers).

Buddhists use a form of rosary, called *akshamala* or *mala*. This is a prayer necklace containing 108 pearls. Each pearl represents a mantra, and using it enables Buddhists to keep track of the number of recitations they have made. Mantras are sacred sounds that are chanted for meditation purposes. "*Om mane, padme hum*" is probably the best-known mantra. This mantra, known as "mani" for short, is learned by Buddhist children at a very young age, and is said to contain everything necessary to achieve enlightenment in one sentence. This mantra is usually translated as "the jewel in the lotus."

Walls and mounds of mani stones can be found throughout Tibet. These are stones that have been inscribed with "om mane, padme hum." The largest of these mounds is said to be 353,100 cubic feet in size, and contain more than two billion stones.[9] Buddhists pray as they walk around these mounds in a clockwise direction.

Prayer wheels play an important role in Buddhism. They contain a mantra or sacred text. As the wheel is turned in a clockwise direction, each revolution sends the mantra out and into the world.

---

9. Tatjana Blau and Mirabai Blau, *Buddhist Symbols* (New York: Sterling Publishing, 2003), 230.

Prayer flags serve a similar purpose. They dispense prayers and blessings as they flutter in the breeze.

How Does Prayer Work?

The law of attraction says that whatever it is you admire or desire, you will ultimately get. This works in every area of life. You developed your character because of the way you thought. You even attracted your friends to you. If you are a kind and honest person, you will attract kind and honest people to you. Similarly, if you are dishonest and untrustworthy, your friends are likely to have criminal tendencies. If you focus on prosperity, what happens? In time, you'll become prosperous. Naturally, if you constantly think about what is lacking in your life, you will receive more of that, too.

Prayer works because of the law of attraction. If you want something badly enough, your mind will attract whatever it is you want to you. This works both consciously and unconsciously. Consequently, as long as your desire and motivation are strong enough, the universe will work on your behalf and attract whatever it is you so strongly desire. Naturally, your belief in the process is essential, too. Jesus said, "Ask, and it shall be given you" (Matthew 7:7).

Prayer enables you to contact the infinite and start the metaphysical process that will bring your desires into being. However, you need to make sure that your prayers are in agreement with your every-day thoughts. If you pray for prosperity but spend the rest of your time thinking and moaning about your lack of money, you will attract more poverty, as that is what you are focused on.

My friend Ken Ring wrote the story of a drifter named Bruce, who spent his life living on the road. Bruce lived a long and happy life, on his own terms, and developed an interesting philosophy. Bruce believed "The world is my church and life is my prayer."[10] Bruce believed his every thought and action was a form of prayer. If everyone thought this way, the world would be a completely different place.

We have looked at different types of prayer, but we haven't answered one very important question: why pray? That is the subject of the next chapter.

---

10. Ken Ring, *Super Tramp: The Story of Bruce* (Auckland, New Zealand: Milton Press, 1999), 251.

two

Why Pray?

I have been driven many times to my knees
by the overwhelming conviction
that I had nowhere else to go.
My own wisdom, and that of all about me,
seemed insufficient for the day.
—ABRAHAM LINCOLN

Surely, if God already knows what we need, why is it necessary to pray? This question has perplexed many religious thinkers over the centuries. St. Thomas Aquinas (1225–74), the Italian theologian and philosopher, came up with an answer that is still highly regarded today. He started with three objections to prayer:

1. God already knows what we desire.

2. Prayers are petitions to God, asking Him to change his mind. However, God is unchangeable.

3. As it is more generous to give to people who don't ask than it is to those who do, and bearing in mind God's generosity, surely it is better not to ask at all.

St. Thomas Aquinas starts by mentioning that God's providence decides not only what events will occur, but also how and when they will occur. St. Thomas proposes that God has decided certain things, such as a miraculous healing, will occur only if people pray for it. When we pray for the desired result, we effectively become partners with God in making it happen. Consequently, when we pray, we do so to remind ourselves of our need for divine aid rather than to tell God of our need. We do not pray in an attempt to change God's mind, but to ask for whatever it is God decides we should have. God already gives us many things without being asked for them. However, God still wants us to pray so we can "gain confidence in God and acknowledge Him as the source of all our blessings."[11]

Immanuel Kant (1724–1804), the German philosopher, had a different answer to the question "Why

---

11. St. Thomas Aquinas, *Summa Theologiae* (London: Eyre & Spottiswoode, 1964), 53.

pray?" He thought that "the purpose of prayer can only be to induce in us a moral disposition; its purpose can never be pragmatic, seeking the satisfaction of our wants. It should fan into flame the cinders of morality in the inner recesses of our heart."[12]

People have prayed throughout human history, and even today, people with no faith at all pray in moments of crisis. This is because, at heart, we are spiritual beings, and we desperately crave a spiritual element in our lives.

Antediluvian people were very much in tune with their environment, and had a strong sense of the sacred. They used prayer to access the spiritual dimension and communicate with their ancestors as well as the architect of the universe. They saw the spiritual and material worlds as being different aspects of the whole, and lived simultaneously in both worlds.

Today, many people ignore the spiritual dimension and focus entirely on the physical aspects of life. Unlike other beings, humans have the ability to communicate with the divine, to gain peace, comfort, hope, understanding, and a sense of purpose. Consequently, as prayer provides all these benefits and much more, prayer works.

---

12. Immanuel Kant (translated by Louis Infield), *Religion Within the Limits of Reason Alone* (New York: Harper & Row, 1960), 182–83.

Another reason to pray is to become closer to God. The aim of prayer is to achieve a union between you and God—and the more conversations you have, the closer this bond will become. The spark of divinity inside you will grow, and create a light that will be sensed, and sometimes even seen, by others.

The more you pray, the more you'll realize that you, along with everyone else, are part of God. Consequently, you'll stop praying to God, and start praying from the divine spark inside you. In reality, as you are God, it is God who is praying.

Prayer also provides immediate benefits to the person who is praying. An exchange of energy between you and the divine provides feelings of positivity and well-being that enter every cell of your body. This can effect healing of mind, body, and soul. Research shows that people who pray are happier than people who don't.[13]

Søren Kierkegaard (1813–55), the Danish philosopher and theologian, wrote a famous maxim that says, "Prayer does not change God, but it changes him who prays."

Mahatma Gandhi (1869–1948) wrote that prayer "brings us an awareness of God, yes, but it also

---

13. David B. Larson and Mary A. Greenwold Milano, "Are Religion and Spirituality Clinically Relevant in Health Care?" Article in *Mind/Body Medicine 1*, no. 3 (1995), 147–57.

nourishes the one who prays, both mentally and physically."[14]

St. Augustine (354–430), one of the early Christian church fathers, wrote, "The very effort involved in prayer calms and purifies our heart, and makes it more capacious for receiving the divine gifts, which are poured into us spiritually . . . there is brought about in prayer a turning of the heart to Him, who is ever ready to give, if we will but take what He has given; and in the very act of turning there is effected a purging of the inner eye, inasmuch as those things of a temporal kind which were desired are excluded, so that the vision of the pure heart may be able to bear the pure light, divinely shining, without any setting or change: and not only to bear it, but also to remain in it; not merely without annoyance, but also with ineffable joy, in which a life truly and sincerely blessed is perfected."[15]

Because of the intrinsic benefits that praying provides, prayer works—even if the prayer itself is not answered. Although not all prayers are answered, there are numerous recorded instances of answered prayers.

---

14. Mahatma Gandhi, quoted in "What's Wrong with Prayer" by Oswald J. Rankin, article in *Rosicrucian Digest*, 1961. Originally published by Rosicrucian Press (San Jose, CA). Reprinted by Kessinger Publishing (Whitefish, MT: 2004), 235–38.

15. St. Augustine, "On the Lord's Sermon on the Mount," in *A Select Library of Nicene and Post-Nicene Fathers*, edited by Philip Schaff (New York: Christian Literature Company, 1886–90), volume 6 (published 1888), 38.

George Müller (1805–98) is a good example. He, and the charitable institutions and thousands of children who were dependent on him, survived for more than fifty years on prayers. He refused to beg or ask for food or other provisions, and on many occasions he had no food whatsoever in his house. However, food always arrived when it was needed. Müller prayed in secret for whatever it was he and his dependents needed. The people who gave him money always said they'd felt an uncontrollable urge to send him a specific sum, and this would always be exactly what he needed at the time.

George Müller started working with orphans in 1836 when he and his wife made room in their own home for thirty girls. By 1870, more than two thousand children were being looked after in the five homes Müller provided. At the same time he did this, Müller was also financially supporting 150 missionaries. The George Müller Foundation is still carrying on charitable activities, and it obtains funds through prayer, rather than any other form of fund-raising.[16]

Another example shows the power of group prayer. Bishop Thomas Bowman was attending a conference in Mount Vernon, Ohio. During the conference, Bishop Janes told the attendees that Bishop

---

16. George Müller, *The Life of Trust, Being a Narrative of Some of the Lord's Dealings with George Müller* (London: James Nisbet and Company, 1864). A shorter version was published in the United States by Gould and Lincoln (Boston, 1870).

Matthew Simpson was dying, and asked them to unite in prayer. During the prayer, Bishop Bowman felt suddenly reassured, and afterward told another person present that he was certain Bishop Simpson would not die. He mentioned this to the others, and thirty attendees told him they felt exactly the same. Several months later, Bishop Bowman happened to meet Bishop Simpson, and asked him what he'd done to regain his health. The bishop replied that he did not know, and his physician had proclaimed it a miracle. One afternoon, when his condition was critical, his doctor left for thirty minutes. When he returned, he noticed an astonishing improvement. Bishop Bowman asked for more details, and discovered that the improvement had occurred at the exact time he, and his colleagues, had been praying.[17]

In the early 1990s, the Spindthrift Research Group in Salem, Oregon, performed extensive research on the power of prayer. In an early experiment, they soaked rye seeds in salt water and then planted them in a container of vermiculite. This container was divided in half by a length of string. Either one side or the other was prayed for, and the germinated seedlings were counted. This was repeated numerous times. In each case, the seeds that were prayed

---

17. Matthew Simpson, "Absent Treatment by Prayer." Article in Walter Franklin Prince, *Noted Witnesses for Psychic Occurrences* (New Hyde Park, NY: University Books, 1963), 295–96.

for sprouted more abundantly than the seeds in the other half of the container. This experiment demonstrated that prayer worked.

After this, they performed more tests to see if they could measure a difference between directed and nondirected prayer. A directed prayer is one in which a specific outcome is sought, such as remission from an illness. A nondirected prayer asks the universe for God's will to be done. They found that both methods worked, but nondirected prayers were more effective. The Spindthrift team came to the conclusion that when we pray, we should retain a "pure and holy" consciousness of the person or object we are praying for, but not ask for a specific outcome.

Masaru Emoto in Japan performed a series of experiments, which he recorded in his book *The Hidden Messages in Water*.[18] These experiments explored the effects that thoughts, words, and music have on water. One photograph in his book shows a frozen water sample from the lake at Fujiwara Dam. The water appears dark and amorphous. Another photograph shows what the same water looked like after Reverend Kato Hoki, the chief priest of the Jyuhouin

18. Masaru Emoto, *The Hidden Messages in Water* (Hillsboro, OR: Beyond Words Publishing, 2004); *The Message from Water III: Love Thyself* (Carlsbad, CA: Hay House, 2006); *Water Crystal Healing: Music & Images to Restore Your Well-Being* (New York: Atria Books, 2006); *The Shape of Love: Discovering Who We Are, Where We Came From, and Where We Are Going* (New York: Doubleday, 2007).

Temple, prayed over it. The change in the water is astonishing, and the second photograph shows a beautiful, bright, clear hexagonal crystal within a crystal. The first photograph showed no crystals.

As we humans are largely water, Mr. Emoto's experiments should interest everyone, as they demonstrate that thoughts have the power to influence and change water.

No matter what your definition of prayer may be, prayer can help you make valuable changes in your life, revitalize and restore your faith, and guide you on your path in this lifetime.

three

Magic and Prayer

I was awakened to the knowledge that I possessed
a magical means of becoming conscious of and satisfying
a part of my nature, which had up to that moment concealed
itself from me. It was an experience of horror and pain,
combined with a certain ghastly terror,
yet at the same time it was the key to the purest and holiest
spiritual ecstasy that exists.
—ALEISTER CROWLEY, *THE CONFESSIONS*
OF ALEISTER CROWLEY

Magic and prayer have been interconnected for thousands of years. Both deal with the realm of the unseen, and are concerned with effecting change in the world. The magician causes this to occur by demanding the change he desires. The priest achieves the same result by beseeching the gods for whatever it is he wants. The ancient Egyptians practiced both magic and religion, and it was often difficult to determine which category a specific act belonged to. The

Greek and Roman writers made no attempt to separate magic and religion. They found it impossible to define magical prayer, as it covered everything from lucky charms to mystical philosophy.

It is still difficult to define magical prayer today, especially as the prayers of many religions contain elements of magic in them—though this fact is frequently downplayed or denied. Prayers involving ritual, repetition, incantations, kissing, incense, candles, and wine are intrinsically magical. There is nothing wrong in this, as all prayer is helped when accompanied by an element of magic.

The main difference between magic and a religious ritual is that magic is always performed with a specific goal in mind. This is often the case in religious ritual also, but it's not essential. Someone may, for instance, pray to a god, without necessarily asking for anything in return. A magician never performs a spell without desiring something in return.

Magic in Jewish Prayer

Magic has always played an important role in Judaism. Daniel is called "master of the magicians, astrologers, Chaldeans, and soothsayers" (Daniel 5:11). Moses ranks as one of the greatest magicians of all time.

God revealed His secret name to Moses when God told Moses, "I AM THAT I AM" (Exodus 3:14). I AM is YHVH, the magical name of God, which was so sacred it could be said by the high priest in the Holy of Holies only once a year, on Yom Kippur. This name could not be spoken after the destruction of the Temple in 70 CE. An alternative name, ADONAI (LORD), could be spoken in prayer, but even today many Orthodox Jews prefer to use the word *Hashem* (the Name). All of this shows how sacred the name of the creator of the universe is, and what an honor and privilege it is even to know it. For a Jew, saying God's name is the most powerful magic there is.

Jewish prayer played a major role in all of the schools of Judaism. The Merkabah mystics of the first century CE focused on the first ten chapters of the book of the prophet Ezekiel and meditated on his vision of a divine chariot supported by winged beings called *Hayyot.*

In the thirteenth century, the Spanish kabbalists studied the ten sephiroth, or divine emanations. The Kabbalah requires study, prayer, and action. Study involves contemplation and meditation, as well as learning. Prayer includes helping others, and action involves manifesting the divine will in every moment of every day. In other words, life itself becomes a prayer.

The sixteenth-century Lurian kabbalists practiced a mode of prayer taught by rabbi and mystic Isaac Luria (1534–72). This involved meditating on the letters of the divine names before transforming them into prayer.

Eliphas Lévi was the pen name of Alphonse Louis Constant (1810–75), a French magician, occultist, kabbalist, and author who was largely responsible for the revival of ceremonial magic in the nineteenth century. He included a kabbalistic prayer in his book *The Magical Ritual of the Sanctum Regnum:*[19]

> *Be favorable unto me, O ye Powers of the Kingdom Divine.*
>
> *May Glory and Eternity be in my left and right hands, so that I may attain to Victory.*
>
> *May Pity and Justice restore my soul to its original purity.*
>
> *May Understanding and Wisdom Divine conduct me to the imperishable Crown.*
>
> *Spirit of Malkuth, Thou who has laboured and has overcome; set me in the Path of Good.*
>
> *Lead me to the two Pillars of the Temple, to Jakin and Boaz, that I may rest upon them.*
>
> *Angels of Netzach and of Hod, make ye my feet to stand firmly on Yesod.*
>
> *Angel of Gedulah, console me. Angel of Geburah, strike, if it must be so, but make me stronger, so that I may become worthy of the influence of Tiphereth.*

---

19. Eliphas Lévi (translated by W. Wynn Westcott), The *Magical Ritual of the Sanctum Regnum* (London: Redway Press, 1896). This book can be found online at http://www.occult-underground.com/levi.html (accessed 18 March 2009).

O Angel of Binah, give me Light.

O Angel of Chokmah, give me Love.

O Angel of Kether, confer upon me Faith and Hope.

Spirits of the Yetziratic World, withdraw me from the darkness of Assiah.

O luminous triangle of the world of Briah, cause me to see and understand the mysteries of Yetzirah and of Atziluth.

O Holy Letter Shin.

O ye Ishim, assist me by thy Name Shaddai.

O ye Kerubum, give me strength through Adonai.

O Beni Elohim, be brothers unto me in the Name of Sabbaoth.

O Elohim, fight for me by the Holy Tetragrammaton.

O Melakim, protect me through Jehovah.

O Seraphim, give me Holy Love in the Name Eloah.

O Chashmalim, enlighten me by the torchyes of Eloi and the Shekinah.

O Aralim, Angels of power, sustain me by Adonai.

O Ophanim, Ophanim, Ophanim, forget me not, and cast me not out of the Sanctuary.

O Chaioth ha Kadosh, cry aloud as an eagle, speak as a man, roar and bellow.

Kadosh, Kadosh, Kadosh, Shaddai.

Adonai Jehovah, Ehyeh Asher Ehyeh.
Hallelu-Jah
Hallelu-Jah
Hallelu-Jah.
Amen. Amen. Amen.

The person reciting this prayer needs to face east and gaze heavenward. As this prayer progresses, the person saying the prayer progresses through the ten sephiroth of the Tree of Life and then asks different choirs of angels for help.

Magic in Christian Prayer

There is a great deal of magic in Christian prayer, too. In the Gospel according to Mark, we read:

And they bring unto him one that was deaf, and had an impediment in his speech; and they beseech him to put his hand upon him. And he took him aside from the multitude, and put his fingers into his ears, and he spit, and touched his tongue; and looking up to heaven, he sighed, and saith unto him, Eph-pha-tha, that is, Be opened. And straightway his ears were opened, and the string of his tongue was loosed, and he spake plain. And he charged them that they should tell no man: but the more he charged them, so much the more a great deal they published it; and were beyond measure astonished, saying, He hath

*done all things well: he maketh both the deaf to
hear, and the dumb to speak.* (Mark 7:32–37)

In this instance, Jesus was using both magic and
prayer to effect a healing. He was obviously praying
when he looked up to heaven and sighed. The spit-
ting, touching, and strange words are all highly magical. This instance was by no means unique. In the
Gospel according to John, we read how he gave sight
to a man who had been born blind:

*He spat on the ground, and made clay of
the spittle, and he anointed the eyes of the blind
man with the clay, And said to him, Go, wash in
the pool of Siloam, (which is by interpretation,
Sent). He went his way therefore, and washed,
and came seeing.* (John 9:6–7)

Not surprisingly, the early Christian church wanted
to separate the miracles of Jesus from mere magic.
This might explain a curious passage in the Acts of
the Apostles: "Many of them also which used curious arts brought their books together, and burned
them before all men" (Acts 19:19).

For the last two thousand years, Christians have
used relics, novenas, indulgences, rosary beads, candles, icons, and medals to help them in their prayers.
All of these seem more magical than spiritual, but
that is not important as long as they help their own-
ers achieve a closer connection with the divine.

Simple actions, such as making the sign of the cross, appear to perform the dual role of providing protection, while making the person closer to God. According to tradition, making the sign of the cross can save your life, too. When St. Benedict Biscop (c.628–c.689), the Anglo-Saxon clergyman, made the sign of the cross over a drink he had been given, the cup shattered. This was fortunate, as the drink contained poison.

Pater Noster

The Sator Square is a magic square that was popular in Roman times as a protective amulet. The words create a palindrome that reads the same from right to left, left to right, top to bottom, and bottom to top:

```
S A T O R
A R E P O
T E N E T
O P E R A
R O T A S
```

The oldest-known version of this magic square was found in the ruins of Pompeii. Six early examples of this square have been found: two in England, two in Pompeii, and two in Syria. The letters in this square can be rearranged to create a cross that reads PATER NOSTER, the first two words of the Lord's Prayer in Latin. Two As and Os are left over, and these represent Alpha and Omega, referring to Christ as the beginning and the end:[20]

```
            A
            P
            A
            T
            E
            R
A P A T E R N O S T E R O
            O
            S
            T
            E
            R
            O
```

Another interesting discovery was that every T in the magic square is flanked by an A and an O. The Latin capital letter T was one of a number of secret symbols that represent the cross of Jesus.

Different suggestions have been made as to the meanings of the words in the magic square. The most common translation is: "Sator, the sower, holds the

---

20. The Revelation of St. John the Divine says: "I am Alpha and Omega, the beginning and the ending, saith the Lord, which is, and which was, and which is to come, the Almighty" (Revelation 3:8). See also Revelation 21:6.

wheels by his work."[21] The main problem in translating the words is that *Arepo* appears to be a made-up word, and cannot be translated.

Consequently, many people believe the magic square was a secret message that early Christians used to make themselves known to each other. It would be fascinating if this were the case, as this magic square has also been used in folk magic as both a lucky charm and an amulet. In Saxony in 1742, the citizens were ordered to have plates inscribed with the square to act as fire extinguishers.[22]

This magic square is a perfect example of the combination of prayer (*Pater Noster*: Our Father) and magic (magic square).

Candles

A flame symbolizes enlightenment, love, and spiritual purification. Consequently, it is not surprising that fire and flames play a major role in most religions. People in antiquity revered fire, initially as a god and later as a symbol of the power of the divine. In the Bible, God is described as a "consuming fire" (Hebrews 12:29). In the book of Deuteronomy, "people hear the voice of God speaking out of the

---

21. Nigel Pennick, *The Secret Lore of Runes and Other Ancient Alphabets* (London: Rider and Company, 1991), 204.

22. *Encyclopedia of Magic and Superstition* (London: Octopus Books, 1974), 176.

midst of fire" (Deuteronomy 4:33). In the first book of Kings we read: "And call ye on the name of your gods, and I will call on the name of the Lord: and the God that answereth by fire, let him be God" (1 Kings 18:24). Angels had flaming swords to protect the Garden of Eden (Genesis 3:24).

In Judaism, the symbol of the soul is a flame. On the anniversary of the death of a Jewish person, a candle called a *yortzeit* (which means "year time" in Yiddish) is burned for twenty-four hours to symbolize the person's soul. Hanukkah, the Jewish winter festival of lights, commemorates the rededication of the Temple in Jerusalem in 165 BCE. During this festival, one of the candles in the *hanukiyah*, or nine-branched candleholder, is lit each day for eight days to symbolize the survival of the Jewish people. The ninth candle is called the *shamash*, and it is used to light the other candles.

A Jewish woman becomes a priestess temporarily when she lights a Sabbath candle on Friday and says a blessing out loud. After this, she silently asks God to protect her family. Candles are lit at the start and the end of every Sabbath observance. The candle lit at the end is braided and has two wicks, one symbolizing the Sabbath and the other the remaining days of the week. This is the *havdalah* candle.

In Christianity, a flame symbolizes Christ as the light of the world. The Psalmist wrote, "For thou wilt light my candle: the Lord my God will enlighten my darkness" (Psalms 18:28). Catholics light candles for many reasons, including the veneration of saints. On All Saints' Day (November 1st), Catholics around the world light votive candles in memory of the deceased.

Candles are also often lit as a form of prayer. The person may stop praying, and even move away, but the candle will continue burning, effectively carrying on the prayer until the candle has burned out.

Religious artists frequently use the idea of a spiritual flame that burns without destroying or consuming. A flaming heart is the symbol of many saints, including St. Augustine and St. Anthony of Padua. This spiritual flame unfortunately also had a dark side, and many atrocities were committed by Christians purging "evil" with fire.

Candles are used to symbolize the resurrection in the Paschal rituals performed at Easter by both the Roman Catholic and Eastern Orthodox churches. Candles are extinguished and relit. The candles are then blessed, and a prayer recited:

Lord God, Almighty Father, inextinguishable light, Who hast created all light, bless this light sanctified and blessed by Thee, Who hast enlightened the whole world; make us enlightened by that light and inflamed with the fire of Thy brightness; and as Thou didst enlighten Moses when he went out of Egypt, so illuminate

*our hearts and senses that we may attain life and
light everlasting through Christ our Lord. Amen.*

Candlemas is celebrated each year on February 2nd,
originally because this was the feast of the Purification of the Virgin Mary, forty days after the birth of
Jesus. Starting in the eleventh century, this day also
marks the Presentation of Christ in the Temple. A
procession takes place, and the candles that will
be used in the church during the following twelve
months are blessed.

Buddhists believe that when the world was first
created, Adi-Buddha, the first Buddha, appeared
in the form of a flame burning in a lotus flower.[23]
A pillar of fire is sometimes used to symbolize the
Buddha.

In Japan, at the annual Obon festival held over
three days in either July or August, candles and fires
are lit to welcome and honor the spirits of ancestors, who are believed to return to their old homes
at this time. After three days of prayer, dancing, and
feasting, more fires are lit to help the spirits return
to their new home.

Native Americans have considered fire to be a
manifestation of the Great Spirit. Many of them also
call the sun *the Great Fire.*

---

23. Elisabeth Goldsmith, *Ancient Pagan Symbols* (New York: G. P.
Putnam's Sons, 1929), 8–9.

Incense

An inscribed tablet dating back to 1530 BCE refers to the burning of incense in a religious ceremony. The rising smoke from burning incense symbolizes prayers heading upward to heaven, and the scent of incense is intended to put people into the desired altered state that is conducive to prayer. Frankincense and myrrh are two types of incense that have been used for thousands of years. The ancient Egyptians were very fond of incense and used it for both fragrance and religious purposes. Many Egyptian carvings showing kings burning incense are still in existence today.

God ordered Moses to prepare incense: "And the Lord said unto Moses, Take unto thee sweet spices, stacte, and onycha, and galbanum; these sweet spices with pure frankincense: of each shall there be a like weight: And thou shalt make it a perfume, a confection after the art of the apothecary, tempered together, pure and holy: And thou shalt beat some of it very small, and put of it before the testimony in the tabernacle of the congregation, where I will meet with thee: it shall be unto you most holy" (Exodus 30:34–36).

The wise men brought incense as a gift to the baby Jesus: "And when they were come into the house, they saw the young child with Mary his mother, and fell down, and worshipped him: and when they had opened their treasures, they presented unto him gifts; gold, and frankincense and myrrh" (Matthew 2:11).

Incense has always played an important role in Judaism and Christianity. Buddhists use it in their daily prayers, in festivals and celebrations, and as an aid to meditation. They also burn joss sticks to indicate the passage of time. Hindus use it in their rituals. The Chinese honor their household gods and their ancestors by burning incense. In Japan, Shinto rituals frequently use incense. Native Americans burn sweet-smelling herbs in their prayers, and when making offerings to the Great Spirit.

Rosaries

Roman Catholics use strings of beads, divided into groups of ten, to help them count their prayers. These strings of beads are called rosaries. The name comes from the Latin *rosarius*, which means "garland" or "bouquet." Rosaries make it easy to repeat, for instance, ten "Hail Marys" without needing to count them at the same time.

An old legend says the Virgin Mary appeared to St. Dominic (1170–1221), founder of the Order of Friars Preachers, while he was praying for help in dealing with people who were against Christians. When he asked her for a weapon to help him, she gave him a rosary. Because of this, Dominican priests wear a rosary on the left side of their belts, as this is where knights wore their swords.

Unfortunately, this charming story is not true. Muslims introduced rosaries to Christians during the Middle Ages. At that time most people were illiterate, and the rosaries helped them remember prayers and passages from the Bible.

The Greek and Russian Orthodox churches use prayer ropes, which consist of a series of small knots tied on a length of black yarn. The number of knots range from thirty-three to one hundred. The number thirty-three was chosen because each knot represents one year in the life of Jesus.

Muslims use prayer beads in strands of thirty-three or ninety-nine. Ninety-nine beads enable them to pray the ninety-nine names of Allah.

Buddhists and Hindus also use beads to help them count their prayers. These are called *mala* and contain 108 beads.

There are also Jewish rosaries, but they are not used for prayer. Their purpose is to provide something to occupy the hands on the Sabbath and other holy days.

We'll discuss prayer beads and rosaries in much more detail in chapter 17.

Music

Music helps provide an emotional element to prayer, and is frequently used to enhance the experience. Psalms, hymns, chanting, drumming, bells, and singing bowls are all used to help people reach the desired meditative state.

St. Paul gave valuable advice on the subject of music: "Speaking to yourselves in psalms and hymns and spiritual songs, singing and making melody in your heart to the Lord" (Ephesians 5:19).

Language

Words are powerful in both magic and prayer. In the first book of the Bible, we read: "And God said, Let there be light: and there was light" (Genesis 1:3). This appears to indicate that God created everything in the world by pronouncing the name of each thing. Sigmund Freud (1856–1939), the founder of psychoanalysis, said, "Words were originally magic and to this day words have retained much of their ancient magical power."[24]

Sometimes it can be difficult to separate magic and prayer. Arnald of Villanova (c.1235–1311) wrote that a priest had cured him of one hundred warts in ten days. The priest touched each wart and made the sign of the cross over each of them. He then recited the Lord's Prayer, but instead of saying "Deliver us from evil," he said, "Deliver Master Arnald from the wens and warts on his hands." He completed the

---

24. Sigmund Freud, *The Complete Introductory Lectures on Psychoanalysis*, volume 15 (edited and translated by J. Stachey) (New York: W. W. Norton, 1966), 17.

ritual by taking three stalks from a plant and placing them in a damp, secluded location. As the stalks withered and died, so did the warts.[25] This is obviously magic, but it was performed by a priest and used the most famous Christian prayer of all.

Words can be said in many different ways to achieve different effects. A chant that starts quietly, and builds in volume and intensity, creates excitement and anticipation. The choice of words can be important, too. Rhythm, alliteration, and the effective use of pauses also create a powerful effect in the minds of the listeners. These can be used just as well in magic as they can in prayer.

All words possess magical qualities. *Forgiveness*, *love*, and *gratitude* are all words with powerful emotional and magical connotations. These words play an important role in prayer, and are the subject of the next chapter.

---

25. Richard Cavendish, ed., *Man, Myth and Magic* (London: Purnell Books, 1970), 1418.

four

Forgiveness, Love, and Gratitude

Even as a mother protects with her life her child,
her only child,
So with a boundless heart should one cherish
all living beings;
Radiating kindness over the entire world.

—BUDDHA

Forgiveness, love, and gratitude are valuable qualities that play an important role in prayer. We can make our prayers more effective when we utilize all three of these qualities.

Forgiveness

A few years ago, I spent some time in Assisi, Italy, the home of St. Francis (1182–1226). St. Francis is remembered for many reasons. Children are taught about him because of his love for all living things, and his alleged ability to communicate with animals. He was the first person known to receive the stigmata. He saw a seraph, one of the most highly ranked angels. He founded the Franciscan order of monks. I visited Assisi for all of these reasons, but also because St. Francis is credited with writing one of my favorite prayers:[26]

> *Lord, make me an instrument of Thy peace;*
> *Where there is hatred, let me sow love;*
> *Where there is injury, pardon;*
> *Where there is doubt, faith;*
> *Where there is despair, hope;*
> *Where there is darkness, light;*
> *And where there is sadness, joy.*
> *O Divine Master,*
> *Grant that I may not so much seek to be con-*
> *soled as to console;*

---

26. Although this beautiful and famous prayer is attributed to St. Francis, the oldest version of it in its present form was published in *La Clochette* ("The Little Bell"), a French spiritual magazine, in 1912. It was published as an anonymous prayer. A slightly different version of this prayer was included in an Alcoholics Anonymous publication *Twelve Steps and Twelve Traditions*. A hymn version of this prayer, called "Make Me a Channel of Your Peace," has become the anthem of the Royal British Legion. The Missionaries of Charity, the Roman Catholic order established by Mother Teresa, recite this prayer at the start of every day. Although this prayer was probably not written by St. Francis, it is not surprising that it's been attributed to him, as it exemplifies his thoughts perfectly.

> *To be understood, as to understand;*
> *To be loved, as to love;*
> *For it is in giving that we receive,*
> *It is in pardoning that we are pardoned,*
> *And it is in dying that we are born to Eternal*
> *Life.*
> *Amen.*

This prayer does not ask God for anything. In fact, it does the opposite. It asks God to help the person praying become an instrument of His peace. It says, "Where there is hatred, let me sow love," making this a prayer of forgiveness.

In a sermon he delivered at Christmas in 1957, Martin Luther King, Jr. (1929–68), the American minister and civil-rights campaigner, said, "We must develop and maintain the capacity to forgive. He who is devoid of the capacity to forgive is devoid of the power of love. There is some good in the worst of us and some evil in the best of us."[27]

Alexander Pope (1688–1744), the English poet, wrote, "To err is human; to forgive, divine." It sounds simple, but in practice it's extremely hard to do. Over

---

27. Martin Luther King, Jr., preached a sermon called "Loving Your Enemies" at the Dexter Avenue Baptist Church in Montgomery, Alabama, at Christmas in 1957. He started his sermon with these words. He wrote the sermon while in prison for nonviolent civil disobedience during the Montgomery bus boycott. This sermon is available online at http://salsa.net/peace/conv/8weekconv4-2.html (accessed 19 March 2009).

the years, I have met many people who are angry and bitter about events that occurred many years before. Some of these have been major calamities, but others seem so insignificant it's hard to imagine anyone refusing to let go of them. However, some people never let go of a perceived injustice.

One morning in the spring of 1985, Robert Enright, a professor of educational psychology at the University of Wisconsin–Madison, prayed as he drove to work. For some reason, the word *forgiveness* suddenly came to him. This became a life-changing experience, as Dr. Enright and his graduate students immediately started a forgiveness study group.

They began by looking at the oldest stories of forgiveness. These included the Hebrew story of Joseph, who was sold into slavery by his brothers; the Buddhist story of a philosopher who forgave the king who'd had him whipped; and the Biblical story of the prodigal son. Gradually, they developed a definition of forgiveness. They decided that forgiveness was not condoning, forgetting, or reconciling. It took them two years to agree that forgiving occurs when people who have received unfair treatment reduce their resentment and are good to the perpetrators, even if the perpetrators are undeserving.

Since then, Dr. Enright has written or edited four books and more than eighty papers on the subject of forgiveness. He has also performed major experiments in schools in Belfast, Northern Ireland, and

Milwaukee, Wisconsin. Children who participated in these forgiveness experiments experienced huge decreases in anger and hostility.[28]

Dr. Enright discovered that people who felt deeply hurt often suffered from depression, anxiety, anger, and low self-esteem. The act of forgiveness eased all of this. Consequently, the act of forgiveness helps the emotional and physical health of the person who is doing the forgiving. This means that forgiving others for the hurt they have done to you is actually a blessing that you give to yourself.

This may not sound logical at first glance. Surely, if you have been wronged, the person who did it should apologize to you first. There is no guarantee the other person will ever apologize. Is it worth feeling anger and resentment forever? Or is it better to forgive the person, and move on? You have a choice.

Forgiving someone doesn't mean you condone that person's actions. Nor do you need to forget what the person did. Forgiving means you're letting go of whatever it was, and moving forward again.

Forgiveness helps you physically, mentally, emotionally, and spiritually. Forgiveness restores your sense of well-being and personal power. It also nurtures your soul. Most religions place emphasis on forgiveness.

---

28. Kerry Hill, "The Wisconsin Idea. Robert Enright: Planting Seeds of Forgiveness in Belfast and Milwaukee," 25 April 2007. Online at http://www.wisconsinidea.wisc.edu/profiles/Enright/ (accessed 19 March 2009).

In Buddhism, forgiveness is practiced to prevent harmful thoughts and prevent bad karma. Buddhists use meditation, compassion, and loving kindness as techniques to avoid creating difficult situations in the first place.

Christians obtain forgiveness by confessing their sins to God, and by forgiving others. Most Christians believe that Jesus was crucified to forgive the sins of humanity. St. Paul wrote, "Forgiving one another, if any man have a quarrel against any: even as Christ forgave you, so also do ye" (Colossians 3:13). The Gospel according to Mark also includes the words of Jesus on forgiveness and prayer: "And when ye stand praying, forgive, if ye have ought against any: that your Father also which is in heaven may forgive you your trespasses. But if ye do not forgive, neither will your Father which is in heaven forgive your trespasses" (Mark 11:25–26). When Jesus was on the cross, he prayed, saying, "Father, forgive them; for they know not what they do" (Luke 23:34).

Forgiveness plays an important role in Hinduism, too. Atonement and asking for forgiveness is related to karma. Everything you have done in the past and are doing now helps create the conditions in which you'll be living in the future. As hurting others creates negative karma, it is important to ask for forgiveness whenever this occurs.

Islam teaches that Allah will forgive virtually everything. As Islam is a monotheistic religion, Allah will not forgive the worship of other gods or idols unless the sinner recognizes the error of his ways and returns to Allah, in which case all will be forgiven. The Qur'an also tells believers to forgive one another: "The recompense for an injury is an injury equal thereto [in degree]: but if a person forgives and makes reconciliation, his reward is due from Allah: for [Allah] does not love those who do wrong" (Sura 42:40).[29]

In Judaism, if a person sincerely apologizes to the person he or she has wronged and tries to rectify the situation, the person who has been wronged is required, as a good Jew, to grant forgiveness. In Christianity, a person can gain forgiveness from God. In Judaism, the person can gain forgiveness only from the person he or she has wronged. During Yom Kippur (the Day of Atonement), Jews ask God to forgive them for any transgressions they may have made against Him during the previous year.

Henry Wadsworth Longfellow (1807–82), the American poet, expressed forgiveness perfectly when he wrote, "If we could read the secret history of our enemies, we should find in each man's life sorrow and suffering enough to disarm all hostility."[30]

---

29. *The Qur'an.* The version quoted here is published by Tahrike Tarsile Qur'an, Inc. (Elmhurst, NY: 2001, p. 234) and was translated by Abdullah Yusuf Ali.

30. Henry Wadsworth Longfellow, "Table-Talk." Included in *Prose Works of Henry Wadsworth Longfellow* (Boston: Ticknor and Fields, 1857), 798.

The Forgiveness Process

Forgiveness is not always easy. You would not be human if you didn't feel anger and resentment after being humiliated or hurt by someone else. Fortunately, there is a process to help you eliminate the negativity, forgive the other person, and move on with your life.

1. Select the person you wish to forgive.

2. Relax in a quiet meditative state, and think about all the reasons why you need to forgive this person. These reasons might include health, stress reduction, self-esteem, and peace of mind.

3. Visualize the moment when you were hurt. "See" it as if it were on a television screen. Tell yourself, "I'm letting this go now." Visualize the television screen becoming smaller and smaller, and fainter and fainter, until it disappears.

4. Pray sincerely for the person you are forgiving. Visualize him or her as clearly as possible, and imagine this person surrounded by divine light. Ask God to protect and look after this person.

5. Ask God's forgiveness for any hurts you may have committed to others.

6. Conclude by praying in your normal manner. When you have finished your prayers, take a few deep breaths and open your eyes.

7. If you find you are still harboring feelings of resentment or anger toward the other person, repeat this process and continue doing it until all the emotion connected with the incident is gone.

Love

"Love makes the world go 'round" is an old saying that contains enormous truth in it. Without love, few of the great books, songs, or works of art would ever have been produced. Love connects all of humanity, and could well be the most powerful force in the universe. Love can produce indescribable joy and incredible happiness, but it can also create absolute despair and depression. No other emotion has that incredible range or power.

Dictionaries describe love as a strong affection or fondness toward a person or thing. In actuality, it is much more than that. When you truly love someone, you want to do all you can to help that person grow and develop. You accept this person as he or she is, without trying to change him or her.

You, along with everyone else on this planet, want to be loved. For this to happen, you must love yourself first. When you accept and love yourself, you can start generating love for the special people in your life, and for all humanity. When you encourage, guide, and help someone else, you are expressing a form of love. The person you are helping will feel this love, and

grow and blossom as a result. When you forgive someone for something he or she has done to you, you are
also expressing love. Ideally, you also love your work,
everything else you do, and every person you meet.
If you do this, you'll be following the advice of Jesus,
who said, "Let your light (love) so shine before men,
that they may see your good works, and glorify your
Father which is in heaven" (Matthew 5:16).

Whenever possible, I try to brighten the day of
the people who serve me in stores and restaurants
by making a friendly, positive comment. I might
compliment them on something, such as their service or variety of merchandise. I might comment on
the weather or something that is occurring locally.
It doesn't matter too much what I say, as I'm trying to be friendly and am looking for the good in
the other person. It isn't hard to say a few friendly
words, and I usually get better service as a result. In
a small way, I'm spreading love to humanity, one
person at a time. We all need to get along with other
people, and love for all humanity makes this much
easier to do. Love for humanity, and love for God,
play an essential role in prayer.

Jesus referred to love several times in the Gospels. He told a group of Jews that they had not the
love of God within them (John 5:42). He told his
disciples, "This is my commandment, That ye love
one another, as I have loved you. Greater love hath
no man than this, that a man lay down his life for
his friends" (John 15:12–13). He even told people

to love their enemies (Matthew 5:44, Luke 6:27). St. Paul wrote, "Thou shalt love thy neighbor as thyself. Love worketh no ill to his neighbor: therefore love is the fulfilling of the law" (Romans 13:9–10).

St. Paul also made another astute comment on love: "And we have known and believed the love that God hath to us. God is love; and he that dwelleth in love dwelleth in God, and God in him. Herein is our love made perfect, that we may have boldness in the day of judgment: because as he is, so are we in this world. There is no fear in love; but perfect love casteth out fear" (1 John 4:16–18). When we focus on love, fear and negativity cease to exist.

In Islam, *love* is one of the most frequently used words in the Qur'an, occurring approximately once in every fifteen verses.[31] This includes Allah's universal love as well as a more personal love. Surah 19:96 says, "On those who believe and work deeds of righteousness, (Allah) Most Gracious will bestow love." Surah 3:31 says, "Say: 'If you do love Allah, follow me: Allah will love you and forgive you your sins: for Allah is Oft-Forgiving, Most Merciful.'" There are four types of love in Islam: love for Allah, love for the Prophet Muhammad, love for humanity, and love between a married couple.

---

31. This includes all the different words that could be translated as *love*. These include: *hub* (Allah's warm but selective love bestowed on the just), *mahubba* (service, devotion), *rabb* (sustain, cherish), *rabubiyyah* (universal love), *rafah* (kindness, compassion), *rahim* (mercy, tolerance), *rahmah* (blessing, grace, generosity), and *wudda* (Allah's particular love).

Whenever I think of love, I remember the famous Japanese proverb: "One kind word can warm three winter months."

Gratitude

I used to make my living as a hypnotherapist. I still see a few people every week, but I accept only the cases that seem interesting. One person I saw several months ago is a good example: Laura was a well-to-do widow in her early fifties. She had three children and a grandchild. Laura had suffered from insomnia ever since her husband died seven years earlier. Her doctor prescribed her sleeping pills, but she wanted to give them up as she said they made her feel she was in a daze all the time. While talking to her, I asked her what she thought about while lying in bed at night waiting for sleep.

"I think of Glenn, and how cruel it was that he died so young." She told me that her husband had died in a car crash at the age of forty-five.

"What else do you think about?" I asked.

"Oh, all the bad things that have happened. My best friend and I had a falling out about ten years ago, and we haven't spoken to each other since. My sister moved to Australia, so I hardly ever see her. My father and I had a row just before he died." She spoke for about five minutes, telling me about all the bad things that had happened in her life.

"What about the good things?" I asked when she'd finished.

Laura looked surprised. "Good things? I don't think about good things when I go to bed!"

I suggested that for the next week she should think about all the things she was grateful for. Laura expressed doubt at this idea, especially when I added that she should try to lengthen the list every night.

When she came back the following week, she thanked me for the suggestion.

"I'm still not sleeping without the pills," she said. "But I'm much happier lying in bed thinking good thoughts, instead of bad."

It took a few more sessions before she was able to sleep every night without sleeping pills. Laura was thrilled with that, but she was even happier to discover the number of things she was grateful about.

"I'm looking forward to things again," she said. "And I haven't done that since Glenn died."

Laura had discovered the truth of Professor Michael McCullough's words that "grateful people are happier, more optimistic, [and] more satisfied with their lives. They are more empathetic toward others. We even have a bit of evidence that grateful people are viewed as kinder, more helpful, and more supportive than less-grateful people."[32] Professor McCullough

---

32. Michael McCullough, cited in Jeff Diamant, "Your Mind Tends to Thank You for Feeling So Thankful," *Star-Ledger* (Newark, NJ), 26 November 2003. Quote available online at http://www.wordspy.com/words/gratituderesearch.asp (accessed 19 March 2009).

and his colleagues conducted research into the effects of gratitude at the University of Miami.

Meister Eckhart (c.1260–c.1327), the German mystic, is said to have written, "If the only prayer you said in your whole life was 'thank you,' that would suffice." Although this beautiful quote is attributed to Meister Eckhart, I have been unable to find it in his published works. I first saw it printed in large type on a wall in a drug rehabilitation center I spoke at more than a quarter of a century ago.

Buddha said, "Let us rise up and be thankful, for if we didn't learn a lot today, at least we learned a little, and if we didn't learn a little, at least we didn't get sick, and if we got sick, at least we didn't die; so, let us be thankful."[33]

These two quotes make me realize just how much I have to be thankful for. In our prayers we should express our gratitude to the Almighty for all of the bountiful gifts we have been given, starting with the gift of life itself. We should also express our gratitude to the special people in our lives, for enriching us in countless ways.

As you now know, forgiveness, love, and gratitude all have a major role to play in prayer. We'll learn more about how to pray in the next chapter.

---

33. Buddha, cited in http://thinkexist.com/quotation/let_us_rise _up_and_be_thankful-for_if_we_didn-t/199980.html (accessed 19 March 2009).

five

How to Pray

Prayer is so simple; it is like quietly opening a door and slipping into the very presence of God. There in the stillness to listen to His voice, perhaps to petition or only to listen, it matters not; just to be there, in His presence . . . is prayer.

—Anonymous

Followers of almost every religion are told to pray, but very few people are ever taught how to do it. Even people who pray regularly are not sure they're doing it correctly.

George Washington Carver (1864–1943), the American scientist and humanitarian, wrote, "The trouble is people don't know how to pray. Their prayers don't even reach the ceiling." This is just as true today as it was when he said it.

Amazingly, few churches teach their congregations how to pray. They assume that they already know how to do it, but unfortunately this is seldom the case. Mother Teresa said the best way to learn how to pray is to pray. However, for most people, it is not as easy as that. Even the disciples of Jesus needed help. When they asked him how to pray, he taught them the Lord's Prayer, the most revered prayer in Christianity (Luke 11:1–4).

Pope John Paul II (1920–2005) put it this way: "How to pray? This is a simple matter. I would say: Pray any way you like, so long as you do pray. You can pray the way your mother taught you; you can use a prayer book. Sometimes it takes courage to pray; but it is possible to pray, and necessary to pray. Whether from memory or a book or just in thought, it is all the same."[34]

In chapter 1 we discussed the idea that God is everywhere. With this in mind, when you pray to God, you are in reality praying to an infinitely powerful force that is part of you. You should pray and talk to this presence as if you were one, which, in fact, you are. Ralph Waldo Emerson wrote: "Prayer as a means to effect a private end is meanness and theft. It supposes dualism and not unity in nature and con-

---

sciousness. As soon as the man is at one with God, he will not beg. He will then see prayer in all action."[35]

There is no need to concern yourself with the words you use. Any prayer you make will be the right prayer, as it will be unique to you.

Whenever it's possible, I like to perform some sort of service for someone else two or three hours before my prayers. A Spiritualist minister taught me this many years ago. He said that giving of yourself before praying has a profound psychological effect on the other person, which adds strength to the prayers. Whether or not this is the case, it's a good habit to get into, and I've had many pleasant experiences as a result of doing it.

What to Pray For

Many people seem to think God is a type of cosmic Santa Claus who will provide them with whatever they want, be it a new television or a new relationship. You can pray for "things," and you certainly should ask for help when you need it. You can also thank God for all the blessings you have in your life. Ultimately, though, the real purpose of prayer is to spend time in the company of God.

---

35. Ralph Waldo Emerson, *Self-Reliance in Essays: First Series*. Originally published in 1841. Many editions available. My copy is *Essays and Poems by Ralph Waldo Emerson* (London: William Collins & Sons, 1967), 52.

Making Time for Prayer

Often our busy lives prevent us from praying. It's fascinating that all of us can find time to do things we really want to do. You might be having a busy day, but if a friend phones you and suggests you meet for a coffee, you'll probably find time to meet. You'll also find time to eat, sleep, and pursue a hobby or sport. Why is prayer so often neglected? People want to pray, but seem to fear it at the same time.

Some people feel they can't pray in the present because of their actions in the past. However, the deity you pray to already knows all about you and accepts you as you are. Consequently, if you haven't prayed before, or if you haven't prayed in years, right now is the perfect time to do it. You do not need to wait until you get promoted at work, or enter into a new relationship. Neither should you wait until your life is perfect. Now is a good time to pray, no matter what is going on in your life at this very moment.

As you'll discover in this book, you can pray anywhere, at any time. You can pray while standing in line somewhere, or waiting for the traffic lights to change. You can pray in the bath or shower, or when you are in bed. You can pray anytime you happen to have a few spare moments during the day.

Ideally, you should also have a set time for prayer. If you want to pray, you can find that time. You should pray because you want to pray. It should never seem like a duty or chore. It should be something you look forward to with great anticipation.

When to Pray

Fortunately, you can pray anywhere, at any time. It is helpful to schedule a certain time of day in which to pray, as otherwise days can go by when you think about praying but never find the time to do it. There are ways around this, as you can pray at your desk at work, while waiting for traffic lights to change, or while washing the dishes. However, the ideal time to pray is a designated period when you can focus entirely on your prayer.

You might choose to pray first thing in the morning, or before going to bed at night. These are traditional times of prayer, and many people find it convenient to pray at these times. You might prefer to set aside some time at lunchtime, or get up before the rest of the household so you can enjoy a quiet conversation with God. Any spare moments can be used for prayer.

You can even pray once you're in bed and ready for sleep. If you do this, you'll sometimes fall asleep in the middle of your prayers. This doesn't matter, as your mind will process your thoughts while you're sleeping, and no matter what is going on in your life, you'll enjoy a good night's sleep.

Once you determine the best time of day in which to pray, stick to it until it becomes a habit.

Where to Pray

You can pray anywhere, but it is a good idea to choose a place where you can pray every day, regardless of the season. Many people like to pray in a church, for instance, but this might not be practical in the middle of winter when adverse weather conditions can make it dangerous to venture out. For this reason most people pray at home. If possible, choose a quiet place where you will not be interrupted. If you are fortunate, you might be able to make part of a room your sacred space where you pray. If so, you can decorate this space to make it as welcoming as possible. In time, this space will develop an aura of spirituality, and you'll feel a sense of comfort whenever you are there.

On Your Own or with Others

There are both public and private prayers. When you pray in private, it is a conversation between you and the divine. You are not praying to impress others or to convince others of your piety, but are praying because of your own desire or need. It may sound surprising that people would pray in public solely to impress others, but it has always occurred. Jesus said, "And when thou prayest, thou shalt not be as the hypocrites are: for they love to pray standing in the synagogues and in the corners of the streets, that they may be seen of men. Verily I say unto you, They have their reward" (Matthew 6:5). Most people who pray, pray mainly in private, as there are no constraints. You can pray whenever you wish, without waiting for a service or for others to join you.

When you pray in a group, possibly in a church, synagogue, or mosque, or maybe at a prayer meeting, you and the other people present are all praying for the same goals. The chances are these will be completely different from your own personal goals, and are likely to be related to the needs of a group, city, country, or even the whole world. This type of prayer is valuable, as it shifts your perspective and takes you away from your normal, everyday concerns.

Group prayer has a long history. Early Christians prayed together partly because of the words of Jesus: "For where two or three are gathered together in my name, there am I in the midst of them" (Matthew 18:20).

The major disadvantage of group prayer is that the words are usually written by others, and this can make it harder to establish a connection with the divine. However, the advantages of praying with like-minded people usually outweigh this. A combination of private and group prayer allows you to enjoy the advantages of both.

Posture

It makes no difference what position you take while saying your prayers. You can pray standing up or lying down. You can gaze heavenward or bow your head. You can assume the lotus position if you want to.

I've met a number of people who kneel beside their bed to say their prayers. They do this because this is how they were taught to pray as children. For them, this is the perfect position, as by assuming it they immediately enter the right state of mind in which to pray. However, kneeling is not a particularly comfortable position. Most people find it easier to pray while sitting in a comfortable chair.

You might like to bow your head, or pray with your hands held together. It makes no difference, as long as it feels right for you.

You can pray while lying in bed, too. This allows you to start and finish each day with a prayer.

I find it helpful to close my eyes while praying, but even this is not essential. I frequently pray while out for a walk or driving in my car. Obviously, in these situations, I have to pray with my eyes open.

Silent or Spoken Prayer

You can pray in any manner you wish. Sometimes a silent prayer might be essential, as other people might be within hearing distance. Obviously, you will pray silently if you are riding on a bus or waiting in line. Even in church your personal prayers will probably be said silently. In the privacy of your own home, though, you can pray silently or out loud. You might sing your prayers. Depending on your need, you might even yell and scream. I like to say my prayers out loud whenever possible, as doing so seems, at least to me, to give them more energy.

Length of Prayers

You can pray for as long as you wish. The duration of the prayer makes no difference as far as its effectiveness. A heartfelt prayer lasting fifteen seconds may prove much more effective than a lengthy, repetitious prayer that lasts for an hour or more. That is because the feelings and intention behind the prayer are much more important than its length. It is also extremely difficult to keep your mind focused on praying for lengthy periods. However, some people can do it. Martin Luther prayed for three hours every day.

If you have not prayed before, or if it is a long time since you last prayed, it is probably a good idea to keep your prayers short, at least initially. A minute or two every day will get you into the habit of praying regularly. You can lengthen your prayers, if you wish, as you gain confidence and experience.

When St. Paul wrote, "Pray without ceasing" (1 Thessalonians 5:17), he was not suggesting that you do nothing but pray. He meant that you should carry out your daily activities with God constantly with you. By doing this, your entire existence becomes a prayer.

What Do I Say?

You do not necessarily have to say anything. Norman Vincent Peale wrote that prayer is "thinking about God." A great deal of prayer is quiet contemplation and thought. Rather than worrying about what you are going to say, it is better to enter the desired state of mind and open your heart and mind to God.

You can say anything you wish while talking to the divine. If you know a prayer of any sort, such as the Lord's Prayer, you might say that first, and then carry on telling God about your concerns and desires. You might start by singing a hymn, or reading from a spiritual text.

Some people like to pray in a formal manner, using old-fashioned, or courtly, styles of speech. However, as prayer is, in effect, an intimate conversation with someone you love and who loves you, it is probably better to speak in your normal manner. You will feel more at ease, and express yourself better, if you do this.

Once you have started praying and feel comfortable with it, tell God about your needs and concerns. If you are worried about something or someone, tell

God about it. You should not feel guilty about praying for something for yourself. You are as worthy as anyone else. In fact, most people's prayers are a mixture of selfishness and altruism. It's good to pray for others, but you should definitely pray for yourself as well.

Your prayer is a conversation with the divine. The more you pray, the closer your relationship will become, and you'll look forward to your quiet, intimate moments with God.

Practice Makes Perfect

Prayer is a skill that can be learned. Initially, you may feel you're making little progress, but you'll gradually discover more and more benefits from your daily practice. Over time, you'll gain more and more pleasure and insight from your prayers, and these benefits will be apparent to others as well.

We'll take some more steps toward successful prayer in the next chapter.

six

First Steps in Prayer

When I pray, coincidences happen,
and when I don't pray, they don't.
—WILLIAM TEMPLE

Several years ago an acquaintance of mine asked for a structured program to help her pray. She told me that she had tried to pray on many occasions without success, and she thought a step-by-step approach would help her. Because she seemed sincere, and was extremely insistent, I created a three-week program for her. She found it helpful, and since then I've taught it to many other people. Without exception, they've all found it useful. Some people have shortened the process, allowing three or four days for each step. However, most people find the process works best if they allow a week for each step.

Week One

Once you have become used to praying, you can pray anywhere at any time. However, when you first start it is best to find a quiet place where you will not be disturbed for at least half an hour. Temporarily disconnect the telephone if need be, and make sure the room is pleasantly warm. Wear loose-fitting clothes.

Before starting, choose a word or phrase that you'll use in the prayer. You might decide to use the word that, for you, describes the divine. *God, Universal Spirit*, or *Allah* are all good choices, as long as they reflect your views. You might use a truth, scriptural saying, mantra, or an affirmation. If you come from a Christian background, you might use sayings along the lines of "Jesus loves me," "Be still and let God," or "The Lord is my shepherd." If you are interested in mantras you might say, "Om mane padme hum." Many years ago I saw this mantra printed on a card on the dashboard of a taxi in Singapore. When I commented on it, the driver told me that it meant "Let there be peace on earth." I know this is not the literal translation, but I liked it and frequently use it myself with his version in mind. It doesn't matter what you choose the first time you practice praying, as you can change it at any time if you think of something better.

Sit or lie down comfortably. You might want to cover yourself with a rug, as doing so provides feelings of comfort and security.

Relaxation

The first step is to quiet your mind and relax your body as much as possible. This is a five-step process.

1. Close your eyes and focus on your breathing. Take three deep breaths. Count slowly to three as you inhale, count to three again while holding your breath, and exhale to the count of three.

2. Continue breathing slowly and deeply. Focus on the toes of your left foot, and allow them to relax as much as possible. When you feel they are totally relaxed, allow the pleasant relaxation to drift into your foot. When your left foot feels totally relaxed, repeat the process with the toes on your right foot, followed by the foot itself.

3. Once both feet feel completely relaxed, focus on your left foot again and allow the relaxation to drift into your ankle and up and into

your calves and thighs. Repeat with the right leg.

4. When you feel both legs are completely relaxed, allow the relaxation to move up into your abdomen and chest. Allow your shoulder muscles to relax. Like everyone else, you carry stress and tension in your shoulder muscles, and they may take longer to relax than the muscles you have relaxed so far. Give them as much time as they need to relax completely.

5. Once your shoulder muscles feel relaxed, allow the relaxation to drift down your left arm and into your hands and fingers. Repeat with the right arm.

6. Your arms, legs, and body are now fully relaxed. Allow this relaxation to drift up into your neck and into your face. Allow the muscles around your eyes to relax as much as possible, and then let the relaxation drift up to the top of your head.

7. You should now feel totally relaxed throughout your entire body. Mentally scan your body to determine if any areas are not as relaxed as they could be. Focus on them until they let go and relax.

8. Take a slow, deep breath, and exhale slowly. Take another deep breath, and as you exhale, silently say the word or saying you chose

before starting. Continue taking slow, deep breaths and repeating your word or phrase, for as long as you wish. You are likely to find that your mind wanders at times. This is perfectly normal. There is no need to be concerned when this occurs. All you need do is return to your word or saying.

9. Stop when you can no longer prevent your mind from wandering, or you sense you've said your word or saying for long enough. Finish by silently saying, "Thank you," or possibly "Amen."

10. Lie quietly and allow yourself to gently return to the here and now. When you feel ready, open your eyes, stretch, and get up.

If possible, spend a few minutes thinking about your prayer session before carrying on with your day. You may have a sense of inner knowing that you've been in direct contact with the divine. You may have doubts about the entire exercise, or experience a variety of reactions between these two extremes. Record any insights that may have come to you during your prayer. You should also record how you felt, both before and after praying. If you were angry or upset before the session, record that, and also record how you felt afterward. If you still felt stressed or emotional afterward, it is unlikely that you allowed yourself to become completely relaxed. Total relaxation is essential, at least for the first few weeks, or until you find you can enter into a prayerful state quickly and easily.

No matter what you felt about the exercise on this first occasion, repeat it once a day for a week. If possible, repeat it at the same time every day. You will find after a day or two that you'll look forward to this quiet time in your day. Even if you fail to make contact with the divine, you'll benefit from the peace, quiet, and relaxation. As the week goes on, you'll find it becoming easier to relax and reach the ideal meditative state. You'll also find that you'll be able to concentrate on your word or thought for longer periods of time. You may experience a moment or two of complete stillness, and a sense of oneness with the Creator. All of this will bring a sense of peace and calm to every aspect of your life.

Week Two

After praying for one week, you'll have gained confidence in the practice. In the second week you're going add one more element to the prayer. After repeating your word, mantra, or saying for a couple of minutes, stop and silently tell the divine that you are ready to establish a closer communication. Enjoy the pleasant peace and stillness, and know you're in the presence of God. Concentrate on your breathing and silently wait to see if you receive a message.

The hardest part of this is to still your mind and wait expectantly. When your mind starts intruding, as it will, gently dismiss it and again silently tell the divine you are waiting for a message.

You may be fortunate and receive a message the very first time you ask for one. However, that is unusual. Wait for as long as you can and then thank the divine for being with you. End the session by expressing your thanks or saying "Amen."

You may find that you have received a message without noticing it. When you carry on with your day, a thought might suddenly appear in your mind, or you might get a feeling that all is well in your world.

Regardless of what happens the first time you ask for a message, continue doing it for seven days. You may, or may not, receive a message on any of these days, but despite this, your connection with the divine will be becoming closer and closer. Patient waiting is an essential element of prayer. Remain patient, because one day, probably when you've given up all hope of ever receiving one, you'll receive a message.

Week Three

Now it's time to start a conversation with the divine. Think about whatever it is you wish to discuss before starting to pray. Once you are totally relaxed, say your keyword or saying for a minute or two, and then mentally make your request or ask a question. Focus on your breathing for a minute or two and see what thoughts come into your mind. You may receive an answer, but it's more likely that you'll experience a sense of peace and the knowledge that your request is being attended to.

If you do receive an answer, you can carry on with the conversation for as long as you wish. No matter what response you receive, you should always finish by thanking the divine for listening.

Problems with Praying

The biggest problem most people have is keeping their minds on their prayer while they are praying. Our active minds sometimes thwart all attempts at prayer, no matter how urgent the need or desire for prayer may be. Even Dr. John Donne (1572–1631), the metaphysical poet and dean of St. Paul's Cathedral, experienced this. In a sermon he gave at the funeral of his friend Sir William Cockayne in 1626, John Donne said:

> *I throw myself down in my chamber, and I call in, and invite God, and his Angels thither, and when they are there, I neglect God and his Angels, for the noise of a fly, for the rattling of a coach, for the whining of a door.*[36]

---

36. John Donne, LXXX Sermons, 1640, no. 80. There are many editions of John Donne's sermons, including *The Showing Forth of Christ: Sermons* (New York: Harper & Row, 1964).

The best remedy for this is to gently bring your thoughts back to your prayer, and to keep doing so as often as necessary until you have finished praying.

Problems Establishing a Connection

Everyone is different. Some people make a strong connection with the divine the first time they sit down to pray. Others take a day or two, or maybe a week. Some people spend weeks trying to establish a connection, and finally give up in disgust.

Fortunately, there is an exercise that will enhance your closeness to the architect of the universe.

1. Go through the relaxation process you have been using before praying.

2. When you feel totally relaxed, think of the most beautiful scene you can remember. You can imagine a beautiful, magical scene if you wish. It doesn't matter what you choose, as long as the scene is clear in your mind and is peaceful and tranquil. Everyone is different. Some people can "see" a scene clearly in their minds, while others sense it in different ways. The way you experience the scene is perfect for you.

3. Once you get a clear impression of the scene in your mind, add other sensations to it. If you're on a beach, for instance, you might feel

the sand beneath your feet and smell the sea spray. You might hear seagulls, and enjoy the warm sun on your skin. Experience the scene in as many different ways you can.

4. Start walking through your scene. There is no hurry, so you can pause and admire the scene whenever you wish. If you chose a beach, you might walk up a sand dune to see the view from a different vantage point. You might leave the beach and walk over grass and into a grove of trees. Again, it makes no difference where you go and what you do.

5. After exploring the scene you are in, choose somewhere to sit down and relax. You might find a park bench, a grassy bank, or perhaps a swing. Look around and marvel at the perfection and beauty of God's creation. You experience a sense of wonder at the magnificence of the world, and as you do, you feel a oneness with the creator of the universe.

6. In your mind's eye, you stand up and walk again until you find yourself at the crest of a small hill. You look all around and gasp at the beauty of the scene. You look upward and watch a beautiful sunset. Soon it is dark, and the moon and stars appear. Again you marvel at the incredible beauty of God's creation. You feel a sense of oneness with God and all

creation, and emotion floods through you as you realize all of the bounties He has created for you.

7. You sit down and say a prayer of thanks to the creator of the universe. You feel incredibly happy, as you know you can return to this transcendent state anytime you want to.

8. You can continue with this visualization for as long as you wish. When you are ready to return to your everyday life, focus on your breathing, and take three slow, deep breaths before opening your eyes.

9. Repeat this visualization on a regular basis, changing the setting if and when you wish. Each time you do this, your connection with the divine will increase, and you'll find it much easier to pray.

Evaluating Your Progress

Obviously, your praying has been successful if you experience a direct communication with God. However, your results can also be measured in other ways. Ask yourself if your relationships with everyone are smoother and more harmonious than before. Are you looking at the wonders of nature with greater awareness? Are you experiencing joy, happiness, compassion, love, and harmony in your life? When you allow the divine spark inside you to surface, you will experience much more peace, success, and contentment in your life.

Continue with your daily prayers as you read the next chapters. Many people find it helpful to write their thoughts on paper before saying their prayers. We'll discuss this process in the next chapter.

seven

Writing Your Prayers

My task which I am trying to achieve is
by the power of the written word,
to make you hear, to make you feel—
it is, before all, to make you see.
That—and no more, and it is everything.
—JOSEPH CONRAD

Writing is an extremely effective way of praying. Writing forces you to focus on whatever it is you are trying to communicate. For many people, putting words on paper is the one of the few ways they have to express difficult thoughts, feelings, and emotions. Consequently, it is particularly useful at times when it's hard to pray, or when you want to pray but find it difficult to get started.

Exercise One—Word Association

For this exercise you'll need a few sheets of blank paper, a pen, and a watch or a clock. Think of the word *prayer*, and allow yourself two minutes to write down all the words that come to mind when you think about this word. If you come from a Christian tradition, the words you choose are likely to be different from those selected by, say, a Muslim.

Here are two examples from attendees at one of my workshops. One young man wrote: *request, appeal, help, God, heaven, church, message, need, heartfelt, urgency, hope.* A middle-aged woman wrote: *forsaken, bewildered, lost, worry, hopeless, love, Mary, angel, saint, God, God, God.*

Once you have written down all the words you can think of in two minutes, stop and look over your list. Think about why you chose the words you did. All of these words are somehow connected to your thoughts and feelings about the word *prayer*. Most of the time they'll show a pattern of thought. The lady in the second example started off with five negative words, which appear to show that her prayers have never been answered. However, once she wrote down the word *love*, her words became more positive, and the "God, God, God" at the end is, in effect, a prayer.

In actuality, you are praying when you do this exercise, as you're putting all your thoughts and energies into the words that come to you when you think of prayer. This puts you in touch with the spiritual side of your nature.

If possible, date and keep your list, and repeat this exercise every now and again. These lists will become a record of how your views on prayer change and develop over a period of time.

Exercise Two—Your Prayer Journal

A prayer journal is a record of your prayers over a period of time. It also reflects your thoughts and feelings about your spiritual life. Because of this, you should buy an attractive blank book to write in. You could use an exercise book or record your thoughts on computer, but an elegant and attractive book is a pleasure to hold and write in. It will become a cherished, and spiritual, possession. You might want to purchase an attractive pen that you use solely for writing in your prayer journal.

This book is for your own thoughts and prayers. You may add other people's thoughts and prayers from time to time, but its main purpose is to record your hopes, fears, dreams, and spiritual progress. Because of this, your book will become increasingly valuable to you, and you'll be able to go back and read about your spiritual journey whenever you wish.

I like to date my entries, but that is entirely up to you. I date my entries, as I keep my prayer journal on an irregular basis. I write in it only when I have something I want to record. Consequently, I might write in it every day for a week or two, and then not make another entry for a month.

Most of the time I record my thoughts and feelings about my prayers, rather than the prayers themselves. I record the names of the people I am praying for, too. Sometimes I sit down to write a few words and end up writing several pages. The exact opposite can also occur. I might think I have a great deal to record, but then I find that a couple of sentences convey everything I want to include.

I consider writing in my prayer journal to be a form of prayer. While writing in it, I'm focused on the task of evaluating and recording my thoughts and feelings about what is going on in my life, and the lives of people close to me.

Exercise Three—Asking Questions

Most of the time I write in my prayer journal after saying my prayers. However, there are times when I deliberately choose to write in my journal before, or instead of, saying my prayers. We all have problems and challenges in our lives. If I need divine help to handle these, or to provide further insight, I'll write my concerns in my prayer journal. I write down everything I can think of that relates to the concern, and finish by asking God a question.

Let's suppose you are concerned about your teenage daughter and her new friends that you don't like or trust. You might write:

Dear God, I'm worried sick about Jessica, and her new friends. Jessica and I can't even have a conversation anymore without it turning into a blazing argument. I know she's a good girl, and has a good brain, but I'm concerned that she might be led astray, as her new friends seem to me to be a bad influence on her. They lack motivation, and sit around all day doing nothing. They're slovenly, and I'm scared they might be on drugs. I need Your help. How can I express my fears and concerns to Jessica in a way that won't upset her?

Having written down your concerns, you can put your journal away and go to bed confident that God will work on your concern. You will probably enjoy a good night's sleep, too, as you've passed all your concerns over to a higher power.

The answer to your question may come in the form of a dream, or possibly a thought that pops into your mind. It could even be an emotional response in which you suddenly feel that everything will work out the way it should. It may come in a different or slightly unusual way.

I remember a client of mine telling me about the difficulties she was having with her four-year-old son.

A day after asking for divine help, she met a friend at a local coffee house. She watched a young mother and her obstreperous son at a nearby table, and saw how this mother handled a potentially difficult situation. She tried the same technique with her son, with excellent results. Universal spirit had somehow arranged this serendipitous moment to teach my client what she needed to know.

You might have occasions in which you need an instant answer. Again, focus on your concerns while writing your thoughts and feelings in your journal. Finish by asking Infinite Intelligence for help in resolving the situation.

Place your journal on your lap, close your eyes, and take three slow, deep breaths. Relax your body using the method described in the previous chapter. When you feel completely relaxed, ask your question, silently or out loud. Wait for an answer. It will come, probably in the form of an intuitive flash in your mind. Express your thanks, become aware of your surroundings, take a few slow deep breaths, and open your eyes. If the situation is urgent, obviously you will have to attend to it first. If you have time, though, write the answer you received in your journal while it is still fresh in your mind.

Exercise Four—Pros and Cons

You can ask questions in another way as well. Start by writing down your concern, and then list all the pros and cons concerning it. If, for example, you have not been talking to an old friend because of a major disagreement, you would list all the reasons why you should establish contact again, and all the reasons why you should not. Once you have done that, write down what you think the outcome would be in each scenario. While you are doing that, you should also write down your feelings about the situation. You might, for instance, feel your friend was at fault, and should apologize to you. Pride may prevent you from making the first move toward reconciliation.

Put your journal aside, close your eyes, and ask the divine to help you resolve the situation. You may, or may not, receive immediate guidance, but you'll feel better about the situation after performing this exercise. Read your lists of pros and cons again, and see if anything occurs to you that could be added. Continue asking for guidance on the matter in your regular prayers, until the matter is resolved.

Exercise Five—Writing a Letter to God

Writing a letter to God is an excellent way to ask for spiritual guidance. Start your letter by writing "Dear God." Naturally, you should use whatever name you choose for the divine. Follow this by writing down your concern, and asking for guidance. Make this as complete as possible. Write in a friendly manner, as if writing a letter to a close friend. Conclude by expressing your thanks to the divine for helping you resolve your problem. Tell God that you have let go of your problem, and look forward to a successful resolution.

Other People's Writing

I enjoy writing my own prayers, but I also pray using other people's words. There are many books of collected prayers, and I enjoy reading them and using examples I like in my own prayers. Frequently, this works serendipitously, and I find prayers that express exactly what I'm wanting to say. This also enables me to use prayers from a variety of periods in history, and from a number of different traditions.

Over the years, a number of these prayers have become favorites of mine, and I experience a sense of comfort and familiarity as I recite them. The famous prayer of St. Richard of Chichester (1197–1253) is a good example:

> *Thanks be to Thee, my Lord Jesus Christ*
> *For all the benefits Thou hast given me,*
> *For all the pains and insults Thou hast borne*
> *for me.*
> *O most merciful Redeemer, friend and brother,*

May I know Thee more clearly,
Love Thee more dearly,
Follow Thee more nearly,
Day by day.

I don't hesitate to modify them, or update the language, to make them more suitable for my purposes.

I often start my prayers by saying a favorite prayer, and then continue with my own prayers. Every now and again, I've had people tell me that personal prayers should come from the heart, and that it could be seen as a form of cheating to say prayers written by others. I can't see the logic in this. Any form of prayer is good, and if the prayer you are reciting represents what you want to say, you should say it.

Writing Prayers for Later Use

You may like to write your own prayers for different purposes. Whenever it's my turn to say the invocation at my local Kiwanis Club, I write a special grace for the occasion. If a friend or acquaintance is unwell, I'll write a special prayer that I can say for that person. I'll keep it in my pocket, so that I can recite or read it whenever I have a spare moment.

I know people who have written special morning and evening prayers that they say every day. These prayers are personal to them, and the fact that they have written them themselves adds special power to the prayers each time they are said.

If you intend to write your own prayers for special occasions, you may want to buy an attractive book to record them in. I have lost many prayers by writing them on scraps of paper that eventually got lost or accidentally tossed out. By recording them in a special book you will ultimately create a powerful book of prayers, each of which has special meaning for you.

Adapting Prayers

You may find a prayer that you like in a prayer book. Many people are reluctant to change these in any way, thinking that the prayer has to be said exactly as it's printed. In fact, the opposite is the case. You should alter and change prayers to fit you and your needs at any given time.

You can also choose prayers from other traditions and change them so they apply to you. Here's an example of a Christian-based prayer, followed by the same prayer adapted for Pagan use:

Dear God: Thank you for all the blessings in my life. For the gift of health, loved ones, and the abundance all around me. For giving us your son, Jesus, so we might all enjoy everlasting life. And thank you for caring about me. Amen.

Earth Mother: Thank you for all the blessings in my life. For the warmth of the sun, the smiles of friends, and the abundance of the earth. For

*the beauty all around us and the joys of each
season. Thank you for giving me life. Blessed be.*

Your Personal Quote Book

Betsy, a good friend of mine, has a beautiful book in
which she writes prayers, quotes, and passages from
favorite religious works. She gains great pleasure
from browsing through her book, and always finds
a passage that relates to whatever is going on in her
life at that moment. Betsy is a student of religion,
and her book contains selections from many sacred
texts. These include:

Buddhism

The Dhammapada: This book contains 423 aphorisms
    that are attributed to Buddha. The most accessible
    translation is by Thomas Cleary.[37]

Diamond Sutra and Heart Sutra: There are more than
    fifty sutras in the Buddhist tradition. (*Sutra* is
    Sanskrit for "thread.") The best known of these
    are the Diamond and Heart Sutras. The Diamond
    Sutra aims to provide enlightenment by meditat-
    ing on the thought that everything we think is
    reality is actually a projection of the mind. The

---

37. Thomas Cleary, trans., *Dhammapada: The Sayings of Buddha*
    (New York: Bantam, 1994).

Heart Sutra records a discussion Buddha had with his followers, and covers the topic of emptiness.[38]

Zen koans: The koans are teaching stories, similar to the parables in the Bible. Their aim is to teach Buddhist truths, such as compassion and acquiring wisdom. There are seven main collections of koans. The Wumenguan koans are the most popular ones in the West.[39]

Christianity

The Bible: The Bible is the most sacred text in Christianity. There are many versions available.[40]

The Gnostic Gospels: The Gnostic Gospels were discovered at Nag Hammadi, Egypt, in 1945. They contain fifty-three documents, including the Gospel of Thomas, the Gospel of Philip, and the Gospel of Judas.[41]

The Dead Sea Scrolls: The Dead Sea Scrolls were discovered at Qumran, near the Dead Sea, in 1947. It took a further nine years for the final discoveries

---

38. Edward Conze, John F. Thornton, Susan Varenne, and Judith Simmer-Brown, *Buddhist Wisdom: The Diamond Sutra and the Heart Sutra* (New York: Random House, 2001).

39. Thomas Cleary, trans., *Unlocking the Zen Koan: A New Translation of the Zen Classic Wumenguan* (Berkeley, CA: North Atlantic Books, 1997).

40. All the Bible quotes in this book are from the Authorized King James version, first published in 1611.

41. Marvin Meyer, ed., *The Nag Hammadi Scriptures* (New York: HarperOne, 2007).

to be uncovered. The Dead Sea Scrolls are some-times considered controversial, as they frequently contradict the gospels and writings of St. Paul.[42]

The Apocrypha: The Apocrypha is a collection of Jew-ish religious writings that were excluded from the original Bible. It includes such well-known books as the Book of Tobit, the Wisdom of Solo-mon, and Ecclesiasticus. Most of the Apocrypha (with the exception of 1 and 2 Esdras, and the Prayer of Manasseh) is included in the Roman Catholic Bible.[43]

The Book of Mormon: In 1827, in Palmyra, New York, Joseph Smith uncovered the golden plates contain-ing the Book of Mormon. This sacred book of the Church of Jesus Christ of Latter-Day Saints tells the story of the lost tribes of Israel, the Jar-edites and Lamanites, who came to America. The Jaredites perished, and the Lamanites fought the Nephites. Mormon and his son were the only survivors. In this book, Mormon tells how Jesus Christ appeared in America after his resurrection and ascension.

---

42. Geza Vermes, trans. and ed., *The Complete Dead Sea Scrolls in English* (London: Allen Lane, 1997).

43. David Daniell (introduced by), *The Apocrypha: Translated out of the Greek and Latin Tongues Being the Version Set Forth AD 1611 Compared with the Most Ancient Authorities and Revised AD 1894* (Oxford University Press and Cambridge University Press, 1895; reprinted by The Folio Society, London, 2006).

Confucianism

I Ching: The I Ching, or "Book of Change," is comprised of sixty-four hexagrams, made up of broken and unbroken lines. It was originally a divination system, but evolved into one of the most important books in Chinese thought. Confucius is believed to have written a commentary on the I Ching, which turned it into a philosophical system.

Analects of Confucius: The Analects of Confucius are a collection of conversations between Confucius and his disciples. Although the style of writing is terse, there is enormous wisdom in the words.

Hinduism

The Vedas: The Vedas date back some 3,500 years, and were first written down in about 600 BCE. Although they are difficult to read, the four books of Vedas (*Rig Veda, Sāma Veda, Yajur Veda*, and *Atharva Veda*) are the cornerstones of Hinduism.

Bhagavad Gita: The *Bhagavad Gita*, or "Song of the Lord," describes the conversation between Krishna, the incarnation of Vishnu, one of the three main Hindu gods, and Arjuna, a warrior, at the time of a fierce battle. The Bible is the most translated sacred text, and the *Bhagavad Gita* is the second most translated.

Upanishads: The Upanishads are sometimes called *Vedanta*, which means "the end of the veda." This is because the Upanishads, although usually published separately, are the final part of the Vedas. There are more than two hundred Upanishads, although most books contain 108.

Islam

The Qur'an: The Qur'an is the sacred book of Islam, and contains the words of Allah that were revealed to Muhammad over a period of twenty-two years. The Qur'an contains 114 chapters, known as Suras.

Judaism

The Talmud: The Talmud is a sacred work in Judaism, and it is considered a religious duty to study it. There are two Talmuds: the Jerusalem (or Palestinian) Talmud and the Babylonian Talmud. Both books are commentaries on Jewish oral law known as *mishnah*.

Kabbalah

The Kabbalah: The Kabbalah is a collection of Jewish mystical writing that has the transcendence of God and higher consciousness as its goal. It teaches that life is an illusion. Jewish legend says angels taught the Kabbalah to Adam, the first man. Another legend says the Kabbalah was part of the oral law given to Moses on Mount Sinai.

The Zohar: The *Zohar*, or "Book of Splendor," is the central part of the Kabbalah. It contains several books that are thought to have been written by Moses ben Shem-Tov de León in the late thirteenth century.

Taoism

Tao Te Ching: The Tao Te Ching is an ancient Chinese work attributed to Lao Tzu. It was originally part of an oral tradition, and was first written down in the third century BCE. The oldest copy in existence dates back to about 200 BCE. It is a short work of eighty-one brief chapters containing wisdom on how to lead a happy and successful life. The information is just as relevant today as it was two-and-a-half thousand years ago.

Writing your prayers is usually something done in the privacy of your home. In the next chapter we'll discuss how you can pray when you're out in the world performing your usual, everyday tasks.

eight

Out-and-About Prayers

*Practical prayer is harder on the soles of your shoes
than on the knees of your trousers.*
—Austin O'Malley

It is of course possible to dance a prayer.
—Glade Byron Addams

An old Jewish saying says, "Any natural act, if hallowed, leads to God." This means you can pray anywhere, at any time. I enjoy walking, and whenever possible I go for a walk every day. This gives me plenty of time to say silent prayers, and it also enables me to make a quick prayer for people I happen to see. I usually say something along the lines of: "Mother, Father, please bless, guide, and be with this person. Thank you."

It is extremely rewarding to make silent prayers for strangers. I frequently receive beautiful smiles in return, and sometimes I exchange a few words with the people I have prayed for.

On one occasion I was traveling by bus and prayed for all the passengers. I made a special prayer for an elderly lady a few seats in front of me. She seemed weighed down with problems and looked sad and worried. As soon as I'd finished my prayer, she looked around and smiled at me. I was pleasantly surprised, and happy to notice that she looked much happier on the rest of the trip.

You can even pray while driving in your car. Ideally, leave a few minutes earlier than you would normally, so you can drive in a calm and relaxed fashion. When you get into your car, sit behind the wheel and take three slow, deep breaths before starting the engine. Tell yourself that your ride will be a spiritual experience, and say a few prayers as you drive to your destination. You'll find that you'll drive safely, and arrive at your destination feeling relaxed after an enjoyable drive.

You can enter the stillness while waiting at traffic lights, or experiencing delays of any sort. Waiting in line is no longer a frustrating delay if you use it to pray. You may, in fact, welcome the enforced pause because of the opportunity it gives you to spend a few moments in prayer.

Something else you can also do when you travel a regular route on a daily basis is to create different prayers for places you pass. For instance, if you pass a hospital, you could say a brief prayer for the patients, doctors, and nurses. When you pass a school, you might pray for the teachers and students. A street name might remind you of a friend or acquaintance. Say a prayer for that person. More than forty years ago I was the first person to arrive at the scene of an accident, and I was able to get help for the family trapped inside their car. I always say a prayer for motorists whenever I pass the scene of this accident.

Pilgrimage

A pilgrimage could be considered a walking prayer. It is a physical, and metaphysical, journey to seek the sacredness of life. The person undergoing the pilgrimage is usually on his or her way to a spiritual or healing place, such as Lourdes, Mecca, or the Holy Land. A Christian might make a pilgrimage to Jerusalem. A member of the Roman Catholic Church might prefer to make a pilgrimage to Rome. A Muslim would make a *hajj*, or pilgrimage, to Mecca. A Tibetan Buddhist would choose Lhasa, Tibet. People go on pilgrimages for many different reasons, such as education, healing, penance, or to express gratitude.

A pilgrimage can be undertaken alone or with others. Geoffrey Chaucer's book *The Canterbury Tales* tells the story of twenty-nine pilgrims who travel from the Tabard Inn, in Southwark, London, to the shrine of Thomas à Becket at Canterbury Cathedral. To make the long walk more enjoyable, they agree to tell stories on the way.

A pilgrimage does not necessarily involve travel. In *The Pilgrim's Progress*, John Bunyan's hero traveled metaphorically "from this World to That which is to Come: Delivered under the Similitude of a Dream, wherein is Discovered the Manner of his Setting Out, his Dangerous Journey, and Safe Arrival at the Desired Country."[44] In *The Pilgrim's Progress*, Christian, the hero of a dream the author is relating, reads that the city he and his family live in will be consumed by fire. He consults Evangelist, who tells him to flee. As he is unable to persuade his wife and family to come with him, Christian leaves alone and makes a pilgrimage to the Celestial City. On his way, he passes through many places, including the Slough of Despond, the Valley of Humiliation, and the Valley of the Shadow of Death. The second part of *The Pilgrim's Progress* was published six years later, and

---

44. This is the full title of John Bunyan's classic allegory, *The Pilgrim's Progress*. It was first published in 1678, and revised editions appeared later that year, and in 1679. The second part of *The Pilgrim's Progress* was published in 1684. There are many editions available. My copy was published by William Collins, London, in 1966.

tells how Christian's wife, Christiana, and her children make the same pilgrimage.

Pilgrimages are not necessarily lengthy journeys carried out in the mind or on foot. I have an oracle tree in a nature reserve close to my home. An oracle tree comes from the Celtic tradition. It is a tree that you agree to look after, and in turn the tree provides you with strength and support when you need it. I enjoy conducting rituals beside my oracle tree. Many years ago, after I had spoken about my oracle tree at a lecture, one of the people in the audience told me that each time I visited my oracle tree I was, in effect, making a pilgrimage, as I was visiting my own personal sacred space.

Labyrinth

A labyrinth might look like a maze, but in reality it is a quest. Labyrinths date back some four thousand years, and were created to help people on their search for transformation and spiritual meaning in their lives. As you walk the labyrinth to the center and out again, you're effectively on a quest for the divine. It becomes a walking prayer.

The word *labyrinth* comes from the Greek *laburinthos*, which means "double-headed axe." The word comes from the Greek legend about Theseus and his battle with the half-human, half-bull Minotaur of Knossos. King Minos imprisoned the Minotaur in the center of huge complex of mazes built at the Palace of Minos in Crete. Theseus fought and killed the minotaur in the middle of this labyrinth.

Labyrinths can also be found at many sacred sites, including Chartres Cathedral and Amiens Cathedral in France, and San Vitale in Ravenna, Italy.

The labyrinth at Chartres Cathedral was built around 1200 CE, and people walk it in hopes of developing their spirituality and gaining a closer connection with God. Many people who were unable to make a pilgrimage to Jerusalem walked the labyrinth instead. Consequently, this labyrinth was sometimes called the *Chemin de Jerusalem*, or "Road of Jerusalem." People seeking repentance sometimes complete the more than two-hundred-yard-long labyrinth on their knees.

Two beautiful modern labyrinths can be seen at Grace Cathedral in San Francisco. The outdoor labyrinth is made of terrazzo stone, and the indoor one is limestone. Christ the King Lutheran Church in Torrance, California, also contains a striking labyrinth.

Daniel, a good friend of mine, makes his own labyrinths on a regular basis, and also teaches people how to make them. He finds the process of constructing a labyrinth to be just as spiritual as walking it.

"I get into a quiet, meditative mood when I first think about making one," he told me. "The mood lasts while I find the space and gather the stones I'll be using. Then I seem to go even deeper into myself while I'm making it. It's a feeling of bliss, really. Time stands still and I get lost in the process. People talk to me and I don't even hear them, as I'm so involved. When I've finished, I always sit down and gaze at it for several minutes. Then, when I feel ready, I take some photos of my work, and do the walk. Walking the labyrinth is a wonderful, spiritual feeling, too, but it's different from the sensations I have while I'm making it. I guess you could say it's all spiritual exercise."

It is not hard to make your own labyrinth, using small stones to mark the path. Ideally, you need about forty square feet of space for your labyrinth. Constructing the labyrinth can be an act of prayer and devotion. In addition to creating a labyrinth, you are also forming a sacred space.

You can even "walk" a labyrinth in a book, using a finger to trace the route in and out. Experiment using your nondominant hand.

Quiet your mind before entering a labyrinth. Use the time inside the labyrinth for meditation, reflection, and prayer.

We are now coming closer to the heart of prayer. Contemplative prayer is the most difficult—and most rewarding—type of prayer. That is the subject of the next chapter.

Contemplative Prayer

We may think of prayer as thoughts or feelings expressed in words, but this is only one expression. Deep prayer is the laying aside of thoughts. It is the opening of mind and heart, body and feelings—our whole being—to God, the Ultimate Mystery, beyond words, thoughts, and emotions.
—THOMAS KEATING

The world can be a noisy place. Everywhere we go we are exposed to loud music, traffic noise, and a wide variety of other man-made sounds, such as television, radio, lawnmowers, and airplanes. Many people, especially those living in large cities, seldom experience true quiet and stillness. Others are afraid of silence. They find it so uncomfortable that they'll turn on the radio or television to create background noise.

Silence is even used as a punishment. People may be ignored or given the cold shoulder because they acted inappropriately. If you are "not on speaking terms" with someone, you are effectively ostracizing him or her. Yet silence can be an enormous blessing in the noisy world we live in today. Blaise Pascal (1623–62), the famous French scientist, wrote in his mystical work *Pensées* (*Thoughts*), "All man's miseries derive from not being able to sit quietly in a room alone."

Isaac of Nineveh (died c.700), a Syrian theologian and author, wrote, "If you love truth, be a lover of silence. Silence like the sunlight will illuminate you in God and will deliver you from the phantoms of ignorance. Silence will unite you to God Himself . . . "[45]

Most of us are always busy, too. We rush from activity to activity with no time to relax. This even applies to people's prayers. As soon as they have finished praying, people immediately rush on to their next task. Their prayers would be much more effective if they finished by enjoying a few quiet moments in the company of the divine. The Psalmist must have known this, as he wrote: "Be still, and know that I am God" (Psalm 46:10).

---

45. Isaac of Nineveh, quoted in *Westminster Collection of Christian Meditations* (Louisville, KY: Westminster John Knox Press, 2000), 190.

Contemplative prayer, frequently called *prayer of the heart*, is a form of prayer that involves waiting quietly and listening for God. Contemplative prayer is, as its name suggests, a combination of prayer and meditation. According to a Gallup poll, people who practice meditative or contemplative prayer experience a more intense experience of God than people who pray in other ways.[46]

However, contemplative prayer requires time and commitment. It cannot be performed in a few minutes. Ideally, contemplative prayer should be practiced for at least thirty minutes at a time, on a regular basis. Few people are prepared to dedicate that amount of time to prayer, which is why contemplative prayer is practiced mainly by people who have dedicated their entire lives to prayer.

Contemplative prayer may seem like a simple process. After all, it is nothing more than spending thirty minutes in silence. In practice, though, it is difficult, as we all have active minds that seldom allow a second to pass without filling it with a thought. Buddhists refer to this as the "monkey mind." Different methods have been devised to help people remain focused on stillness. These include rosary beads and mantras.

---

46.   Margaret Poloma and George Gallup, *Varieties of Prayer* (Harrisburg, PA: Trinity Press International, 1991), 62.

Contemplative prayer can be a powerful and incredible experience. It has a number of benefits, in addition to the obvious one of spending precious moments in the presence of God. You'll gain an increased sense of wonder at the perfection and mystery of the universe. You'll also nurture your soul and feel an increased sense of well-being. Contemplative prayer is also good for your health, because your stress levels and blood pressure will decrease.

There are a number of ways to approach contemplative prayer.

Three Breaths Exercise

This exercise takes only a few seconds, and can be done at any time, anywhere. All you do is pause in whatever you are doing, and take three slow, deep breaths. Think a positive thought with each breath. You might, for instance, say to yourself: "I smile with each breath, feeling calm and relaxed, gaining energy and tranquility."

Whenever possible, close your eyes while doing this exercise. You'll be amazed at the difference a few slow, deliberate breaths, accompanied by positive thoughts, can make to your life.

Contemplative Prayer Exercise One

1. Start by following the first seven stages of the relaxation exercise in chapter 6.

2. Take three slow, deep breaths. Remain aware of your breathing and visualize a peaceful scene. When you are able to sense this scene as clearly as you can, take another slow, deep breath and enjoy the silence. I usually say to myself at this point a phrase from the *Book of Common Prayer* that I remember from my school days: "The peace of God which passes all understanding. May it be with you, and remain with you, now and forever." Several people have told me they feel an indescribable feeling of love at this point. If you experience this, or any other sensation relating to peace or spirituality, focus on it.

3. Wait silently and expectantly. You might imagine yourself going to a quiet place deep within your soul. You might imagine yourself experiencing God's love in every cell of your body. Repeat a mantra or a comforting phrase, if you feel the need.

4. Every time a random thought comes into your mind, gently dismiss it. You might imagine yourself placing the thought onto a fluffy cloud and watching it drift away. If your peaceful scene involves a stream or river, you might place the thought onto a leaf and let it be carried away by the water. If you're on a beach, place the thought onto a wave and let

it drift away. Realize that it is perfectly natural for unwanted thoughts to come into your mind. There is no need to get agitated or think you are incapable of entering the desired meditative state. Simply detach yourself from your idle thoughts, and let them go in any way you wish. Once you have done that, direct your mind back to peace and quiet. Try not to think, reason, or analyze. Simply be. Let go of everything, and allow yourself to spend time in the presence of God.

5. Stay as long as you can in this meditative, contemplative, and expectant state. You may find a few minutes are all you can manage when you first experiment with this.

6. When you feel ready, take three slow, deep breaths, allow yourself to become familiar with your surroundings, say thank you to God, and open your eyes.

7. Spend a few minutes thinking about your time of prayer before carrying on with your day. Write down any thoughts or insights that came to you during, or immediately after, your prayer.

8. Repeat as often as possible. Five times a week would be ideal, if you can manage it.

Contemplative Prayer Exercise Two

This second exercise is called a breath prayer, as it involves focusing on your breath. Breath symbolizes God's breath of life, which He used to create the first man (Genesis 2:7). Not surprisingly, breath is considered a symbol of life. Controlled breathing is used in Buddhist, Hindu, Muslim, and Tantric meditation. Breath has always been related to the spirit, and it is considered a divine gift that is returned to Infinite Spirit at the time of death.

1. Start by following the first seven stages of the relaxation exercise in chapter 6.

2. Take three slow, deep breaths. Continue breathing slowly, and focus on each inhalation and exhalation. Whenever your mind wanders, and it will, gently bring your focus back to your breathing. Enjoy the sense of stillness.

3. You'll gradually notice feelings of calmness and total tranquility in every part of your mind and body. You'll find yourself breathing more slowly, and you may feel you're in the presence of the divine.

4. Stay in this state for as long as you wish. Your ever-active mind will tell you when it's time to return.

5. Take three slow, deep breaths. Become aware of your surroundings, say thank you to God, and open your eyes.

6. Think about the experience you have just had for a minute or two before getting up. Write down any insights or feelings you've gained during the exercise.

7. When you feel ready, carry on with your day.

Contemplative Prayer Exercise Three

This third method adds a phrase or mantra to the breath prayer. For the purposes of explanation, we'll use the well-known Jesus prayer, which is sometimes called the prayer of the heart. This prayer is: "Lord Jesus Christ, Son of God, have mercy on me, a sinner." There are longer and shorter versions of this prayer. In this exercise we'll use a shorter version: "Lord Jesus Christ, have mercy on me, a sinner." If you prefer, you might use "Om mane, padme hum," or another phrase or passage of scripture that feels right for you. Alternatively, you might like to repeat your name for God, or use a short word or phrase, such as *love, peace,* or *vibrant health.*

1. Start by following the first seven stages of the relaxation exercise in chapter 6.

2. Take three slow, deep breaths. On the fourth breath, think the words *Lord Jesus Christ* as

you inhale, and *Have mercy on me, a sinner* as you exhale. Continue doing this with each breath.

3. After a few minutes, you may notice the words fading away. Your breathing will slow down, and you'll feel a sense of calmness and peace throughout your body.

4. Stay in this state for as long as you wish. Many people fall asleep at this stage, which is not surprising, since repeating a mantra over and over is a great way to relieve stress and to achieve total relaxation.

5. When you feel ready to return to your everyday life, take three slow, deep breaths, become aware of your surroundings, give thanks to God, and open your eyes.

6. Spend a few minutes thinking about the experience before carrying on with your day. Record any thoughts, insights, or feelings you gained during your time of prayer.

Contemplative prayer takes time to master. In fact, it can even be a struggle at times for people who have experienced it many times before. I know many people who have tried it and given up without ever experiencing the pure joy that comes from spending time with the divine. Experiment with it. Even Thomas Merton, the Catholic mystic, wrote, "Meditation is sometimes quite difficult. If we bear with hardship in prayer and wait patiently for the time of grace, we may well discover that meditation and prayer are very joyful experiences."[47] If you find contemplative prayer difficult, carry on with your other prayers and come back to it at a later date. It takes time, patience, and practice.

Time in the Wilderness

For thousands of years, people have gone to nature to find peace and quiet. In fact, you don't need to travel hundreds of miles to do this. You can find peace and tranquility while sitting in a public park, and even in your own backyard. Sit or walk quietly, enjoying the sounds and colors of nature. I enjoy walking barefoot on grass and sand. For some reason, this seems to intensify my relationship with nature and brings me into a naturally meditative state that often leads on to prayer.

---

47. Thomas Merton, *Contemplative Prayer* (New York: Doubleday, 1990), 34. Originally published as *The Climate of Monastic Prayer* (Kalamazoo, MI: Cistercian Publications, 1968).

ten

Kahuna Prayer

All things considered,
it is my conviction that the kahuna lore
is something which offers us so much of enlightenment
and value that we cannot afford to ignore or neglect it.
—MAX FREEDOM LONG

The Kahunas of Hawaii practiced a powerful form of magic known as *Huna*. Huna is a system that enables anyone to live in harmony with the earth, and to achieve his or her goals. Using this system, the Kahunas were able to perform instantaneous healings, control the weather, read minds, and perform a wide variety of miracles. Our knowledge of this system is due entirely to the work of just one man.

In 1917, Max Freedom Long, a young American schoolteacher, was working on the Big Island of Hawaii. He enjoyed listening to the stories told by the native people. Every now and again, people would mention the Kahunas, but when Long asked questions about them, everybody went silent. He was able to learn a few details by reading, and he learned that the Kahunas had been important people until the Christian missionaries arrived. After that, they were outlawed.

After three years on the Big Island, Long went to Oahu and visited William Tufts Brigham, the curator of the Bishop Museum in Honolulu. Long fully expected to be disappointed yet again, but Dr. Brigham was thrilled to meet him. He had spent most of his eighty-one years studying the Kahunas, and was delighted to meet someone else with similar interests. Long studied with Dr. Brigham until the old man died four years later. Long stayed in Hawaii for a further five years, trying to find the secrets of the Kahunas. Eventually, he gave up. He returned to California and accepted a job managing a camera shop.

Early one morning in 1935, he woke up with the vital thought that enabled him to unlock the hidden secrets. He realized that the Kahunas had to have names to describe the various aspects of their magic. Long immediately began studying the root words of the Hawaiian language.

In his studies with Dr. Brigham, he had learned to look for three important things:

1. There had to be a consciousness directing the process of magic.
2. There had to be some type of force.
3. There had to be some type of substance through which the force could act.

It took Long less than one year to determine the first two, but it took another six years to discover the last one. Long dedicated the rest of his life to researching and promoting Huna. He wrote many books, including *The Secret Science Behind Miracles*.[48] Max Freedom Long died in 1971, just one month short of his eighty-first birthday.

What Is Huna?

Huna is a Hawaiian word meaning "secret." It describes the psycho-religious methods the Kahunas used to create their special form of magic.

The basic concept of Huna is that we all possess three minds, or selves, in the one body. Max Freedom Long called these the low, middle, and high selves. The Kahunas called them the *unihipili* (low self), *uhane* (middle self), and *aumakua* (high self).

---

48. Max Freedom Long, *The Secret Science Behind Miracles* (Los Angeles: Kosmon Press, 1948).

Modern psychology would call them the subconscious, conscious, and superconscious minds.

The Kahunas visualized these three selves as existing in separate parts of the body. The low self was situated in the solar plexus. The middle self was in the left side of the head, and the high self was situated above the head.

The Middle Self (Thinking Self)

We'll start with the middle self as this relates to our conscious minds. This is where we think and make decisions. The middle self is logical, analytical, and interested in setting goals. Because it is the thinking mechanism, the middle self is what most people think of when they refer to themselves.

The Low Self (Feeling Self)

The low self relates to our subconscious minds. It is concerned with feelings and emotions. It makes no conscious decisions. The low self also looks after all the subconscious functions of the body, such as breathing. The low self acts on the thoughts of the middle self. This is why it is so important to think positively whenever possible. If you constantly think negative thoughts, your low self will produce negativity as a result. Naturally, if you focus on positive thoughts, your low self will respond in a healthy and positive manner.

The low self keeps all your memories. Everything you have ever experienced or felt is stored in your low self.

The low self also keeps the middle self informed about information it receives from the senses. Pleasure and pain are good examples.

The High Self (Spiritual Self)

The high self is the spiritual aspect of ourselves. The Kahunas called it the "great parent." It is Mother, Father, and God in one. It is our personal God. Consequently, although it is part of us, it is considered to be separate, which is why it is located above our heads.

The high self is willing to help us whenever we ask for it, but it does not interfere with our free will. The high self is the source of all inspiration, creativity, and intuition, as well as perfect, selfless love.

The Kahunas prayed to their high selves rather than to God. They had no concept of a single, powerful, omnipotent God. Instead, like the mystics, they believed God was inside each of us. It was this belief that they were gods that enabled them to manifest anything they wished.

Every person's high self is connected with every other high self, creating a form of universal mind. It is this that enables us to pray for anything we desire. All we need do is ask.

Aka

Our three selves are surrounded by an invisible substance or aura called *aka*. This aka body creates connecting threads between our low, middle, and high selves. Each time one self contacts another, the bond is strengthened, ultimately creating a strong braid-like connection that enables all three selves to work together in perfect harmony.

The Kahunas believed everything is surrounded by aka. Even our thoughts are surrounded by it. Consequently, we are constantly creating new aka connections. Every time we meet someone, we create a connection. We create connections to the places we visit, and with every thought we make. Thoughts and feelings travel through these invisible aka threads also. This explains how a mother can tell how her child is feeling, even though her child might be many miles away.

We all change as we progress through life. This means we sometimes need to sever aka connections with people and places that were important to us at one time. However, we can never cut the aka links to family members, as there are karmic implications. If you cut these, you will have to repeat the lessons later on.

Mana

Mana is the breath of life. It is the vital life force, or divine spiritual energy. In different parts of the world, mana is called *ki*, *ch'i*, or *prana*. We absorb mana from our food, and from every breath we take.

The Kahunas used water to symbolize mana. Whenever they needed mana, they would take deep breaths and visualize themselves as fountains being filled to overflowing.

Mana is also created by physical activity. Any form of exertion encourages the low self to create more mana. This is how we get our second wind. Physical activity uses up our supplies of mana, but the low self creates more to give us the energy we need.

Mana gives us the energy we require to perform our everyday tasks. Any excess mana can help us achieve our goals. Conversely, tension, stress, and negativity deplete our supply of mana. Because of this, we are more likely to become ill when we feel discouraged or stressed.

We feel good about ourselves when we are full of mana, as we have all the energy and vitality we need. This helps motivate us to achieve our goals. There is a direct correlation between the amount of mana we have and the amount of good fortune and success we experience.

There are different types of mana. The low self absorbs mana from food, water, and air. This is stored in the aka body and shared with the middle and high selves.

The middle self receives mana from the low self and transforms it into *mana-mana*. This doubles its power and effectiveness. Mana-mana is used to stimulate thought and to send orders to the low self.

The high self needs a supercharged form of mana called *mana-loa*, which enables the high self to manifest anything that is desired. Mana-loa is created during the Huna prayer ritual.

How to Manifest Your Desires

All three selves are involved in manifesting your desires. If you have ever tried to manifest something using solely the force of your will (middle self), you will understand why all three selves are necessary. Simply desiring something (low self) doesn't work, either.

It is important that you use this ritual for good purposes only. Karma is a powerful force. If you use the power of Huna for a negative goal, you will ultimately pay a heavy price for it. Wiccans say that any negative energy aimed at someone else will rebound threefold. Consequently, your motives must be good.

You also need to know exactly what you want. As everyone wants more money, people often use the Huna ritual to ask for, say, one hundred thousand dollars. However, money by itself is useless.

You need to decide what you'd do with that amount of money. Would you pay off your mortgage, buy a new car, go on an overseas trip? Once you've decided exactly what you want, ask for that, rather than a sum of money.

Your desire does not need to be a material one. You might ask for better health, for instance. In this case, you also need to be specific. Think of the specific organ in your body that needs healing, and ask for that.

You might ask for a more harmonious home and family life. If this is your request, think of the causes of the current problems and ask for help in resolving them.

During the prayer rite you will have to express your desire clearly and concisely. Consequently, you should think carefully about what you want before starting the rite.

The Huna Prayer Ritual

Max Freedom Long called this prayer ritual the "Ha Rite." *Ha* means "breath" in Hawaiian. During this ritual you will send a request formulated by your middle self (conscious mind) from your low self (emotions) to your high self (God) through the aka cord. You will accompany your request with an offering of mana to provide the necessary power and energy for your desire to become a reality.

As the Hawaiian Kahunas practiced their rituals in secret, you should conduct this ritual in private. I prefer not to tell people when I'm performing this rite, as I do not want the outcome to be unintentionally affected by the comments of others. Choose a time and place where you will not be interrupted. Wear loose-fitting clothing, and make sure the room is warm but not too hot.

There are six parts to the prayer rite:[49]

1. *Fill your low self with mana.* Stand with your feet about twelve to eighteen inches apart. Stretch. Think about the air surrounding you, and realize it is full of life-sustaining energy. This is mana. Feel it all around you. Take a slow, deep breath. Breathe in through your nose and fill your lungs with as much air as possible. Silently say, "I am filling my body with life-sustaining mana." Hold your breath for a few seconds, enjoying the sensation of having your lungs full of positive mana energy. Exhale slowly. Become aware of the mana surrounding you, and again take another deep breath, holding it for a few seconds and exhaling slowly. Do this four or

---

49. The Ha Rite has been published in many books. One such book is Max Freedom Long, *The Secret Science at Work: New Light on Prayer* (Los Angeles: Huna Research Publications, 1953), 127–36.

five times until you feel your body is full of mana. If you are not sure your body is full of mana, pause for thirty seconds and repeat this step again. Some people like to do this step three or four times to ensure they have all the mana they need before moving on to the next step.

2. *Send the mana to your high self.* After finishing step 1, sit down in an upright chair and close your eyes. Visualize yourself overflowing with mana. You might want to use the Kahuna image of seeing yourself overflowing with water. It doesn't matter what image you use, just as long as you have a clear sense that you possess an abundance of mana energy. You are going to offer this mana to your high self. Once you have a clear picture of this in your mind, visualize an enormous burst of energy coming from your solar plexus, up through your body and out of the top of your head, forming a circle of energy immediately above you. You might see this burst of energy as a burst of water similar to that coming from a firefighter's hose. You might see it as a volcanic eruption. Again, it does not matter what image comes into your mind, as long as you know, without any shadow of doubt,

that you are sending an abundance of mana through the aka cord to your high self.

3. *Make your request (part one).* Now that your high self is full of mana, you can make your request. Get a clear picture of it in your mind and superimpose this image on to the circle of energy above your head. Sense whatever it is you are asking for as a reality. If you have requested a better-paying job, for instance, "see" yourself working in your new position. If your request relates to a health problem, sense yourself fully restored to vibrant good health. It makes no difference how you sense your request. Some people see it, while others feel it, sense it, or even hear it. The most important part of this stage is that you experience a sense of inner knowing that whatever it is you have asked for will come to you.

4. *Make your request (part two).* Visualize your request for as long as you can, and then say your request out loud. It does not matter what words you use, but you must speak in a strong and confident manner. You need to feel and sound absolutely certain that whatever it is you have requested will come to you. You might say, "I desire . . . I want and desire it with every particle of my being. I am asking you, my high self, to make this request a reality."

5. *Give thanks.* Pause for several seconds. Let go of your request and focus on your breathing to quiet your mind. When you feel ready, thank your high self for what it has done for you. Say "thank you" in a confident and positive way. You might say, "Thank you, high self, for granting my request. I am grateful for all your blessings on my life. Thank you, thank you, thank you." If you prefer, you can substitute the words *father* or *mother* for *high self.* Your high self is both male and female, and you can use either name if you wish.

6. *Patience.* The ritual is over once you have given thanks. You may experience a natural high. The Ha Rite is a positive, exciting, and euphoric experience. You may have a sense of inner knowing that your request will be granted. Everyone experiences the conclusion of the rite in his or her own way. Repeat the ritual once or twice a day until your request is granted. Consistency and repetition are essential, as your high self will become confused if your requests waver or become contradictory. This will not be a problem if you have clearly determined your desire before starting.

How Long Will It Take?

Unfortunately, it is impossible to answer this. A friend of mine experienced an instantaneous cure for a painful knee. Doctors had told him he'd have to learn to live with the pain, as there was nothing they could do to help him. However, shortly after performing the Ha Rite for the first time, the pain disappeared and has never returned.

However, it is more likely to be weeks or months before your request is manifested. You need to remain positive and alert to any opportunities that may occur to help you achieve your request. Your high self will not manifest your request out of nothing. However, it will create situations that enable your request to be granted. You need to be alert to seize these opportunities.

Repeat the Ha Prayer Rite on a regular basis until your request is granted.

eleven

Creating Your Own
Sacred Space

God speaks in the silence of the heart.
Listening is the beginning of prayer.
—MOTHER TERESA

You can pray anywhere you wish. However, many people like to have a special place where they can meditate and say their prayers. This can be indoors or out. I prefer to perform my rituals outdoors, but this is not possible at certain times of the year. Consequently, I have a sacred space outdoors that I use whenever the weather permits, and I also have a sacred space in my home. Most people prefer to have their designated sacred space in their home.

Ideally, this would be a room in your home. A friend of mine turned her son's bedroom into a meditation room when he left home. Another friend included a prayer room in the house he had built for himself. He calls it his "sanctuary." These people are fortunate in having a designated room for meditation and prayer.

Few people are able to do this, though, and most use part of an existing room. If you have to use an existing room, choose one with as little foot traffic as possible. A bedroom is usually a good choice.

Remember that you can create a sacred space anywhere you happen to be. You can turn a corner of a hotel bedroom into a sacred space, by placing a piece of cloth and a crystal, or another small object, on a coffee table. Many years ago I was given a "traveling Buddha" that is only one inch tall. The original owner of it must have used it to create a sacred space wherever he spent the night.

Ground Rules

If you live with others, you will need to establish some ground rules. The time spent in your sacred space is your private time. This is time you choose to spend entirely on your own, and other members of the household will need to respect this. Make sure that everyone understands that if the door is shut, no one is to bother you. If the phone rings, ask them to take a message. If someone wants to ask you something, they need to wait until you open the door.

Your Altar

You might like to pray in front of an altar. You might have to use part of a dressing table or chest of drawers for this. If you have room for a table to act as your altar, choose one that is aesthetically pleasing. You want everything in your sacred space to be as attractive as possible. A coffee table is usually a good choice, as you can work sitting down. You can consecrate your table to its new task by exposing it for a few hours to both sunshine and moonlight.

North and east are the traditional directions for altars to face, and ideally you should try to place your altar in one of these directions. However, this is not always possible, and you may have to face a different direction.

Choose an attractive altar cloth. Most people choose a white covering, but there is no reason why you can't use a colored one that appeals to you.

You can place spiritual objects such as crystals, candles, a statue of Buddha, or a cross on your altar. You can add anything else you wish. Some years ago I saw a bowl on a friend's altar and asked what it was for. He told me it was his gratitude bowl. Every time he sat down at his altar, he wrote down something on a slip of paper that he was grateful for, and placed it in the bowl. In the course of his prayers, he would thank the divine for whatever it was he had written down and placed in his gratitude bowl.

Ask the other people in your home to leave your sacred objects alone, as they are precious, spiritual objects and must be treated with respect. You also don't want other people's personal energy on them.

Area

You can consider the entire room as your sacred space, or you can decide on part of the room. I have a large circular rug that is approximately nine feet in diameter. I consider the area inside the circumference of the circle to be my sacred space.

This means that when I enter and leave my sacred space, I do it with reverence and respect. I also conduct my prayers, meditation, and rituals inside the circle.

You might choose to use a circle, too. A circle symbolizes unity and eternity. It has no beginning and no end. Circles have traditionally been a sign of protection and signified a holy place. In addition, the circle is sometimes used in Christianity to represent God. No wonder it's frequently called a "magic" circle.

However, you can choose any shape you wish. Naturally, if you are using the entire room, your shape is determined for you by the dimensions of the room.

Another possibility is a square. In Hinduism, the square is considered feminine, and is related to the earth. It represents security, permanence, system, and order. The Kaaba shrine at Mecca is a cube.

My rug indicates the boundaries of my sacred space. You might choose to use an attractive cord, or a selection of small objects, to mark the borders of your sacred space.

Purification

Once your altar has been set up, you need to purify your sacred space. Place a white candle on your altar and light it. If you wish, play some soft, gentle music. Sit or lie down in front of your altar, close your eyes, and relax your body. Think about your purpose in setting up your own sacred space.

When you feel ready, open your eyes and stand up. Walk around and through your sacred space clapping your hands vigorously. If you have incense, walk through the center of your space and allow the incense to cleanse your sacred space. A smudge stick, which you can buy at any New Age or occult store, can also be used to cleanse your sacred space. Recently, I've been experimenting with a smudge spray and am delighted with the results. It is much more convenient and easier to use than a traditional smudge stick.[50]

Sit or lie down again, and close your eyes. Picture yourself in your mind, and visualize a pure white light descending from heaven and surrounding you with protection and divine love. Imagine the white light spreading out to include every part of your sacred space. Say a prayer of thanks, and open your eyes.

Your sacred space is now ready for you to work in it.

Outdoor Sacred Space

I prefer to work outdoors whenever possible. My sacred spaces have always been beside my personal oracle tree. This is a Celtic tradition. The Celts believed that trees acted as bridges between heaven and earth, and because of this could act as mediators between humanity and the gods.

The easiest way to find an oracle tree is to hug trees that appeal to you until you find one that seems to respond to you. You may have to hug a number of trees before you receive a definite response. Some-

---

50. "Smudge in Spray" should be available in most New Age book-stores. It is also available from the manufacturers, the Crystal Garden, Inc. Phone: 1-877-444-5099, or online at www .thecrystalgarden.com or www.smudgeinspray.com.

times I find it hard to decide if I found the tree, or if it found me.

Once you have found your tree, ask it if it would like you to become its guardian. This means you'll become responsible for looking after the tree and the area around it. As you do this, the area will respond and gradually become your sacred space. In return, the tree will provide you with protection, strength, love, and insight.

Your oracle tree will also provide you with healing. Whenever you feel downhearted or depressed, sit down with your back against your oracle tree and allow its healing energies to restore your feelings of well-being and happiness. Talk openly to your oracle tree about any problems or concerns you may have, and listen to the tree's response.

What Should I Do in My Sacred Space?

Your sacred space is a place you can come to whenever you feel the need for peace and tranquility, or if you need a few moments to yourself. Because you have purified it, you should feel calmness and a sense of spiritual awareness whenever you are inside your sacred space.

This makes it the perfect place for praying and meditating. It is also an ideal place for journaling, and for reading spiritual or uplifting books.

Colors in Your Sacred Space

Colors have a profound effect on all of us. Color psychologists have conducted experiments to demonstrate the effects colors have on people. Red, for instance, is popular in fast-food restaurants, as it encourages people to eat quickly and leave. Jail cells painted pink have been used to calm down aggressive prisoners.

Colors can be used for different purposes. I have several altar cloths, thereby allowing me to use a cloth of a specific color that relates to my prayer. I also have an enormous collection of different colored candles that I use. Sometimes I choose my candles purely because I feel like using a certain color. More often, though, I'll choose a candle of the color that relates to my request.

Here are some examples:

Red: provides enthusiasm, energy, vitality, and passion for life.

Orange: aids communication and makes it easier to handle difficult situations. Orange also helps initiate change.

Yellow: provides warmth, joy, and happiness. It is also intellectually stimulating.

Green: provides healing, harmony, stability, and emotional balance. It also aids prosperity.

Blue: provides inspiration, versatility, purity, and the truth.

Indigo: enhances creativity, integrity, wisdom, and spirituality.

Violet: enhances intuition, inspiration, and philosophical and spiritual understanding. It also provides protection.

Pink: relates to love, affection, warmth, spiritual awakening, and healing.

Brown: relates to the earth. Consequently, it is a good color for real estate transactions and creating stability. It is a grounding color.

White: relates to purity, innocence, and the truth. It eliminates negativity and promotes a positive approach to life. Whenever you are unsure about what color to choose, white will work well.

Silver: relates to inner growth, intuition, and artistic work.

Gold: relates to abundance, prosperity, and large-scale undertakings.

Candles

Candles add ambiance and help set the mood for meditation and prayer. You can obviously meditate and pray without candles, but anything that helps create the right atmosphere is beneficial. If you have ever attended a candlelight church service, you will know the special reverence and sacredness candlelight brings.

The number of candles you choose to use is entirely up to you. Sometimes I like the simplicity and purity of a single white candle on my altar. At other times I might choose several candles of different colors. It depends partly on what I'm praying for and my mood at the time.

Prayer Rituals

As this is your own sacred space, you should feel free to do anything that feels right for you. You might kneel down before your altar and pray that way. Alternatively, you might construct an elaborate ritual that becomes an essential part of your spiritual work. You also might choose to do something different every time, depending on your mood and the amount of time you have at your disposal.

Here is a simple ritual that I sometimes use:

1. Start by having a shower or bath. Change into clean, loose-fitting clothes and step into your sacred space.

2. Stand in the center of your space, face east, and close your eyes. Imagine a pure white light descending from heaven and filling you, and your sacred space, with divine protection. When you sense your sacred space is completely surrounded by white light, say "thank you" out loud.

3. Visualize, or imagine, Archangel Raphael is standing in front of you. I picture him as a traveler, holding a staff in one hand and a fish in the other. You might sense Raphael as a whirling, multicolored ball or as pure energy. It makes no difference how you sense Raphael. Once you have a clear impression of Raphael in your mind, say silently or out loud, "Thank you, Archangel Raphael, for your guidance, help, and protection."

4. Turn to face south. Visualize, or imagine, Archangel Michael standing in front of you. I see him as a young man dressed in full body armor. One foot is resting on a dragon, and he wields a sword in one hand and a set of scales in the other. Once you can sense Archangel Michael in your mind, say, "Thank you, Archangel Michael, for your strength, courage, and protection."

5. Turn to face west. This time, visualize Archangel Gabriel as clearly as you can. I see Archangel Gabriel as a traditional angel with large white wings and a kindly face. Say, "Thank you, Archangel Gabriel, for being God's messenger. Thank you for all your help and protection."

6. Turn to face north. Visualize, or sense, Archangel Uriel in your mind. I see him as a strong-looking man with wavy hair. Say, "Thank you

Archangel Uriel, for providing tranquility, peace of mind, and divine protection."

7. You are now completely surrounded by the four main archangels who will protect your sacred space while you pray.

8. Make yourself comfortable in front of your altar. You might choose to kneel, sit, or lie down to pray. Once you feel completely comfortable, relax all the muscles of your body.

9. When you find yourself in a totally relaxed, meditative state, say your prayers or enter the silence to make a contemplative prayer.

10. Take three slow, deep breaths when you have finished praying, become aware of your surroundings, and open your eyes. Stay in your sacred space for as long as you wish, thinking about your prayers and the divine.

11. Stand up, and thank the four archangels in turn. Face east and thank Raphael. Once you have done that, face south and thank Michael, and complete the circle with Gabriel and Uriel.

12. Leave the circle. Your ritual is over.

This ritual is based on one created by the Hermetic Order of the Golden Dawn, a famous mystical and occult society that was established in 1888. Members of this order start their rituals with what they call the Qabalistic Cross. After visualizing the circle, or sacred space, filling with white light, they reach up with their right hands and symbolically pull the white light down. They continue this movement by making a sign of the cross on their bodies by touching their forehead, navel, and each side of their chest while saying, "For thine" (while touching the forehead), "is the kingdom" (while touching the stomach), "the power" (touching the right side of the chest), "and the glory" (touching the left side of the chest). After this, they place both hands over their heart while saying, "forever through the ages." They finish the cross by extending their arms on each side to simulate a cross.

I almost always include the Qabalistic Cross, as it immediately puts me into the desired state of mind. Experiment with it, and use it if you find it helpful. You might come up with other ideas to make the ritual your own.

Now that you have created your own sacred space, it's time to look at you, as you are the person who'll be using the sacred space. We'll do that in the next chapter.

Praying with the Body

*Our own physical body possesses a wisdom
which we who inhabit the body lack.
We give it orders which make no sense.*
—Henry Miller

Your body is a precious physical instrument that
should be looked after and cherished. In addition to your physical body, you also possess a subtle
body, or aura, which surrounds you. The chakras are
energy centers situated alongside the spinal column
inside the subtle body. The word *chakra* comes from
an ancient Sanskrit word and means "wheel." This is
because people who can see them say they look like
revolving wheel-like circles of energy. In the East,

they are often depicted as lotus flowers, a circle surrounded by petals.

People have worked with chakras in the East for
thousands of years, but it was not until the 1970s
that Western scientists started investigating them.
At that time, Dr. Hiroshi Motoyama of Japan conducted research to prove or disprove the existence
of chakras. The results of his investigation were
included in his book *Science and the Evolution of
Consciousness: Chakras, Ki and Psi*.[51]

It's wonderful that scientists have discovered
chakras exist, but most people have experienced the
effects of different chakras at different times in their
own lives. For instance, when you open up your heart
to someone, you can feel it in the area of your heart.
If you surrender your personal power, voluntarily
or involuntarily, you can feel it in your solar plexus.
Our chakras play an important role in our physical,
emotional, mental, and spiritual health.

Root Chakra

Color: red

Desire: physical contact

The root chakra is located at the base of the spine.
It is responsible for survival, self-preservation, physi-

---

51. Dr. Hiroshi Motoyama and R. Brown, *Science and the Evolution
of Consciousness: Chakras, Ki and Psi* (Brookline, MA: Autumn
Press, 1978), 93–98.

cal strength, and feelings of security and comfort. The Sanskrit word for the root chakra is *muladhara*, which means "support." This chakra keeps us grounded, or "rooted" to the ground.

Sacral Chakra

Color: orange
Desire: respect and acceptance

The sacral chakra is situated at the level of the sacrum in the small of the back, approximately two inches below the navel. This chakra is concerned with the fluidic functions of the body, and is responsible for our sexual energy. This includes our relationships with others, as well as the sexual act itself. The sacral chakra is also related to creativity and emotional balance. It provides feelings of optimism and positivity.

Solar Chakra

Color: yellow
Desire: to understand

The solar chakra is situated just above the navel at the level of the solar plexus. The Sanskrit word for the solar chakra is *manipuraka*, which means "jewel of the navel." This chakra looks after our mental perceptions and is responsible for self-esteem, happiness, personal achievement, and an optimistic, positive approach to life. This chakra is our source of personal power. It is also related to digestion and physical well-being.

Heart Chakra

Color: green
Desire: to love and be loved

The heart chakra is located in the center of the chest in line with the heart. It is concerned with relationships, feelings, love, harmony, understanding, higher consciousness, and the sense of touch. When we are "in touch" with someone, our heart goes out to that person. This chakra is also involved with compassion and respect for self and others. When our heart chakra is balanced, we find it easy to express our emotions positively and compassionately.

Throat Chakra

Color: blue
Desire: inner peace

The throat chakra is situated at the level of the throat. It relates to creativity, communication, and self-expression. It also relates to integrity and expressing our own personal truth. When this chakra is balanced, we experience contentment, peace of mind, and a strong faith.

Brow Chakra

Color: indigo

Desire: to be in harmony with the universe

The brow chakra is situated in the forehead, between the eyebrows. It is sometimes called the "third eye." The Sanskrit word for this chakra is *ajna*, which means "command." This chakra looks after the mind, and in many ways can be considered the command center that controls the other chakras. It is involved with insight and the intellect, as well as psychic perception. The brow chakra increases our understanding of the everyday world by making us aware that we are essentially spiritual beings experiencing a physical incarnation. This chakra enhances our intuition and enables us to sense other people's feelings and moods.

Crown Chakra

Color: violet

Desire: universal understanding

The crown chakra is situated at the very top of the head and is the strongest energy center of the body. Artists sometimes depict this chakra as a halo. The tonsure of monks began as a way of exposing this area. The Sanskrit word for crown chakra is *sahasrara*, which means "thousand." The symbol of this chakra is the thousand-petaled lotus.

This chakra enables us to understand the inter-connectedness of all living things. It also harmonizes the interior and exterior sides of our natures. It is our connection to the universal life force. When all the chakras are properly balanced, this chakra provides wisdom and enlightenment.

The Chakras in Other Traditions

The chakras play an important role in Hinduism, but they also appear in many other traditions, often in a hidden or disguised form. In Christianity, Jesus made an intriguing comment that appears to mention the brow chakra, or third eye. In the Sermon on the Mount, he said, "The light of the body is the eye: if therefore thine eye be single, thy whole body shall be full of light" (Matthew 6:22). Also, in the Christian tradition the heart is related to love, and is considered the most sacred part of the body. This relates perfectly to the heart chakra. The halo that appears around spiritual people in religious art can be related to the crown chakra. In these works of art, the halo sometimes surrounds the whole body, showing the subtle body as an aura.

In the Eastern Orthodox tradition, the existence of chakras is even more obvious. This can be seen clearly in the path to spiritual enlightenment undertaken by the anonymous author of *The Way of a Pilgrim.*[52] He traveled around Russia trying to pray constantly. His endless repetition of the Jesus prayer ("Lord Jesus Christ, have mercy on me, a sinner") gradually shifted his prayer from his mind to his throat, and ultimately to his heart.

There are hints of the chakras in Islamic writing, too. In *The Mystic Rose from the Garden of the King*, there is a seven-story temple of knowledge. In the final paragraph of the book, the author writes, "Turn to thy heart; hidden therein lieth the magnificent Temple of Knowledge."[53]

Color Symbolism

As we saw in the previous chapter, colors have always had meanings. Some, such as red, are obvious. As red is the color of blood, it symbolizes the essence of life. Orange represents fertility and abundance. Yellow symbolizes the mind and the intellect. Green symbolizes love and the emotions. Green was the color associated with Venus, the Roman goddess of love. Blue symbolizes wisdom and limitless opportunities. Purple symbolizes spirituality and faith. Gold is related to the sun and symbolizes wealth

---

52. Anonymous, *The Way of a Pilgrim*. Many editions available. Mine is translated by Helen Bacovcin, and published by Doubleday, New York, 1978.

53. Sir Fairfax L. Cartwright, *The Mystic Rose from the Garden of the King: A Fragment of the Vision of Sheikh Haji Ibrahim of Kerbela* (London: William Heinemann, 1925), 196.

and achievement. Silver is related to the moon and symbolizes intuition, mysteries, and dreams. White is the color of purity, innocence, and divinity. Black symbolizes death and regeneration.

Spiritual Color Symbolism

Color symbolism has always been important in Judaism and Christianity. Ancient Hebrew stories tell how red, blue, purple, and white collectively symbolized God.[54] Each color had its own symbolic meanings. Red symbolized love, surrender, and sin. Blue symbolized honor, nobility, and splendor. Purple symbolized brilliance, grandeur, and transformation. White symbolized purity of heart.

Not surprisingly, these colors are mentioned many times in the Old Testament. Here are two examples:

> *And the Lord spake unto Moses, saying, Speak unto the children of Israel, that they bring me an offering: of every man that giveth it willingly with his heart ye shall take my offering. And this is the offering which ye shall take of them; gold, and silver, and brass, and blue, and purple, and scarlet, and fine linen, and goats' hair, and rams' skins dyed red, and badgers' skins, and shittim*

---

54. Faber Birren, *The Symbolism of Color* (Secaucus, NJ: Citadel Press, 1988), 42.

wood, oil for the light, spices for anointing oil, and for sweet incense, onyx stones, and stones to be set in the ephod, and in the breastplate. (Exodus 25:1–7)

And Mordecai went out from the presence of the king in royal apparel of blue and white, and with a great crown of gold, and with a garment of fine linen and purple: and the city of Shushan rejoiced and was glad. (Esther 8:15)

According to the prophet Ezekiel, God's throne was blue, the color of sapphire, and God Himself appeared in the form of a rainbow:

And above the firmament that was over their heads was the likeness of a throne, as the appearance of a sapphire stone: and upon the likeness of the throne was the likeness as the appearance of a man above upon it. And I saw as the color of amber, as the appearance of fire round about within it, from the appearance of his loins even upward, and from the appearance of his loins even downward, I saw as it were the appearance of fire, and it had brightness round about. As the appearance of the bow that is in the cloud in the day of rain, so was the appearance of the brightness round about. This was the appearance of the likeness of the glory of the Lord. And when I saw it, I fell upon my face, and I heard a voice of one that spake. (Ezekiel 1:26–28)

God obviously liked the color blue, since He told Moses:

Speak unto the children of Israel, and bid them that they make fringes in the borders of their garments throughout their generations, and that they put upon the fringe of the borders a ribband of blue. (Numbers 15:38)

In early Christianity, the Trinity was symbolized by the colors blue, yellow, and red. God the Father was represented by blue, God the Son by yellow, and God the Holy Spirit by red.

Color Meditation

As you have seen, each chakra is related to one of the colors of the rainbow. Because of this, you can nurture all of your chakras by relaxing and breathing in color. This exercise is an eight-step process.

1. Lie down and make yourself comfortable. Place a pillow under your head, if necessary. I prefer to lie on the floor for this exercise. If I lie down on a bed, I'm likely to fall asleep before completing the exercise. To try to avoid this, I usually perform this meditation in a well-lit room, where I am less likely to fall asleep during the exercise.

2. Take three slow, deep breaths. Consciously relax your body, starting at your feet and gradually working your way up to the top of your head. Once you have done this, mentally scan your body to make sure every part of your body is completely relaxed.

3. Visualize yourself surrounded by a clear white light of protection. I like to imagine this white light descending from heaven and covering me like a blanket.

4. Take three slow, deep breaths. On the fourth breath, imagine you're inhaling the color red. It's the most beautiful red you've ever seen. Continue inhaling the color red until you feel the red has spread to every part of your body. Focus on the area of your root chakra (base of your spine), and imagine all the red energy flowing into this part of your body, energizing and revitalizing every cell in that area.

5. Take three breaths of clear air. On the fourth breath imagine you're inhaling the color orange. Allow it to spread to every part of your body, and then imagine it gathering in the area of your sacral chakra (just below the navel).

6. Repeat with yellow, green, blue, indigo, and violet, breathing in each in turn, and imagining the color gathering in the parts of the body related to it.

7. Relax comfortably, knowing that you are a rainbow of color, and each color is nourishing and nurturing your chakras.

8. When you feel ready, take three slow, deep breaths, become aware of your surroundings, open your eyes, and stretch. The feelings of relaxation should remain with you for the rest of the day.

You can also do this exercise sitting down in a straight-backed chair. Keep both feet flat on the ground, and rest your hands, palms upward, on your thighs.

Sometimes, instead of breathing in the different colors, I visualize myself walking through a rainbow, absorbing all of the colors one by one. I use both methods, depending on how I feel at the time.

With practice, you'll be able to do this exercise in less than five minutes. Whenever possible, I take much longer than that, as the entire process is enjoyable, as well as relaxing and stress reducing. However, if I'm busy, I'll take a few minutes to perform this exercise, and I function much better afterward as a result.

Praying with the Chakras

The energy produced by the chakras can be harnessed and used to add strength to our prayers. After all, if we are all God, this energy is, in effect, divine energy anyway.

1. Start by performing the color meditation.

2. Enjoy the sensation of being a rainbow of color, surrounded by pure white light.

3. Think of your prayer request, and imagine it sitting in the area of your root chakra, at the base of your spine. Allow your prayer to be energized by the color and energy produced by the chakra.

4. Imagine your prayer request moving up to your sacral chakra. Again, allow it to become energized by the color and power of this chakra.

5. Imagine your prayer rising up your spine, pausing at each chakra to gain all the energy and power it can.

6. Once your prayer request has been energized by your crown chakra at the top of your head, set it free. Visualize it floating through the white light that surrounds you, and ascending to God.

7. Thank the divine for all the blessings in your life. Take three slow, deep breaths and, when you feel ready, become familiar with your surroundings and open your eyes.

Chakra Prayer of Thanks and Gratitude

You can also use the chakras to help you thank the divine for all the love, joy, and blessings you have in your life.

1. Start by performing the color meditation.

2. Enjoy the sensation of being a rainbow of color, surrounded by pure white light.

3. Focus on the area of your root chakra, and give thanks to God for the stability and security you have in your life. This chakra is also concerned with strength, grounding, and self-preservation. Give thanks for all these blessings.

4. Focus on your sacral chakra and give thanks for your sexuality, ability to love, and for all the relationships in your life. You can also offer thanks for your creative abilities.

5. Focus on your solar chakra and give thanks for your personal power, your self-esteem, your emotions and health.

6. Focus on your heart chakra and give thanks for the love you have for yourself and others.

7. Focus on your throat chakra and give thanks for your compassion and ability to communicate effectively with others. Offer thanks for your peace of mind, too.

8. Focus on your brow chakra and give thanks for your intellect, intuition, and spirituality.

9. Focus on your crown chakra and give thanks for the divine in your life.

10. Focus on your root chakra again and visualize a circle or ball of energy, starting at the base of your spine and moving slowly up to the top of your head. Visualize it expanding above your head and ascending to heaven.

11. Thank God for the precious gift of life, and remain in a calm, still, relaxed state for as long as you wish.

12. When you feel ready, take three slow, deep breaths, become aware of your surroundings, open your eyes, and stretch. Think about the prayer you have just made for a few moments before getting up.

Chakra Prayer of Love

1. Start by performing the color meditation.

2. Enjoy the sensation of being a rainbow of color, surrounded by pure white light.

3. Focus on your heart chakra, and thank it for enabling you to give and receive love.

4. Take three slow, deep breaths and imagine your body filled to overflowing with the color

green, symbolizing the healing and loving energy of your heart chakra.

5. Imagine this green energy filling the room you are in, and continuing on to fill the entire building, street, town, country, and—ultimately—world.

6. Enjoy the sensation of sending out loving energy to the entire world. Thank the architect of the universe for enabling you to spread your love so beneficently to everyone.

7. This is a good opportunity to practice forgiveness. If you wish, at this stage you can say, preferably out loud, "I forgive everyone for any hurtful things they may have done to me, deliberately or accidentally. I totally forgive everyone. I also forgive myself for any harm I may have caused anyone else."

8. Enjoy resting in a world of green for as long as you wish. When you feel ready, give thanks once again and visualize the green energy returning to your heart chakra.

9. If you have time, conclude by performing the Chakra Prayer of Thanks and Gratitude. If your time is limited, finish with the final three steps of this exercise.

Other Methods

There are many ways in which you can use your body to help you pray. We've already discussed walking in chapter 8. Any skillful activity using the body can be used to enter the desired meditative state. Yoga, Chi Gung, and aikido, "the art of peace," are good examples. Dancing is another. Recently, someone told me that dancing feeds the soul. This is certainly the case in India, where dance can be a form of prayer.

A few months ago I attended a Pagan festival to celebrate the change of season. The highlight for me occurred in the evening, when many of the participants danced around a huge bonfire, expressing who and what they are in the universal language of dance. In actuality, the dancing was a form of spontaneous group prayer. It always amazes me when someone tells me that Pagans don't pray. In fact, almost all their rituals include prayer, as you'll see in the next chapter.

thirteen

More Prayer Magic

In heaven who is great? Thou alone art great!
On earth who is great? Thou alone art great!
When thy voice resounds in heaven, the gods fall prostrate!
When thy voice resounds on earth, the genii kiss the dust!

—ASSYRIAN PRAYER

The Christian church, in particular, has always been quick to condemn magic. Despite this, the church is happy to use magic in a variety of different ways. Dion Fortune wrote, "There is no essential difference between sticking pins into a wax image of an enemy and burning candles in front of a wax image of the Virgin."[55]

---

55. Dion Fortune, *Psychic Self-Defence: A Study in Occult Pathology and Criminality* (New York: Samuel Weiser, 1981. First published 1930), 18.

Curses could be considered prayers. Although these are obviously evil prayers, they are prayers nevertheless. In the Bible, the prophet Elisha was heading toward Bethel, "and as he was going up by the way, there came forth little children out of the city, and mocked him, and said unto him, Go up, thou bald head; go up, thou bald head. And he turned back, and looked on them, and cursed them in the name of the Lord" (2 Kings 2:23–24). Two bears came out of a nearby wood and ate forty-two of the children.

No magician today would dream of doing anything like that. This is because they follow the Law of Return: everything they send out into the world returns three times over. If you send love out to the world, you will receive an abundance of love in return. If you curse someone, that curse will be returned to you three times over.

St. Paul caused a sorcerer named Elymas to become blind. He said, "And now, behold, the hand of the Lord is upon thee, and thou shalt be blind, not seeing the sun for a season" (Acts 13:11). Elymas immediately became blind.

In his book *Paul, The Mind of the Apostle*, A. N. Wilson wrote that the attraction of Judaism to the Gentiles was its "superior potency, when compared with the other spiritual systems, of its magic powers."[56] He continued by saying, "Jesus himself was clearly in some senses of the word a magician."[57]

The medieval church maintained prayer was a more powerful form of magic than magic spells and charms. At the same time, the church used salt and water to eliminate evil spirits. Priests also used holy water to bless the sick, encourage fertility, and to protect property and possessions. Holy water is water that has been prayed over. It is believed to possess powerful magical qualities. In 1453, during a storm, the inhabitants of Canterbury, England, ran to the churches to obtain holy water to sprinkle in their homes to protect them from evil spirits and lightning.[58]

Apparently, prayers could be used for any purpose, good or bad. Sir Thomas More wrote that thieves prayed for success before setting out to steal.[59] Dr. Edward Lake wrote in his diary about a "Presbyterian" who prayed for two hours before embarking on highway robbery.[60]

---

56. A. N. Wilson, *Paul: The Mind of the Apostle* (New York: W. W. Norton, 1997), 105.

57. Ibid., 106.

58. Keith Thomas, *Religion and the Decline of Magic* (New York: Charles Scribner's Sons, 1971), 30.

59. Sir Thomas More, *The Dialogue Concerning Tyndale*, ed. by W. E. Campbell (London: Eyre and Spottiswoode, 1927), 168.

60. Dr. Edward Lake, *Diary of Dr. Edward Lake in the Years 1667–1678*, edited by George Percy Elliott, included in *The Camden Miscellany, Volume the First* (London: The Camden Society, 1847), 31.

Prayer was also used to answer questions and to predict the future. A Yorkshire yeoman named Adam Eyre prayed to God, asking Him to decide whether or not he should separate from his wife.[61] Oliver Heywood recorded in his diary the story of a young man in Warley, Yorkshire, who prayed to determine the names of the thieves who had stolen his father's corn. He had a vision in which he saw three men he recognized, and immediately asked the authorities to arrest them.[62]

Magic is the art of creating change using the power of the mind. It could be argued that prayer works in exactly the same way. Magicians usually employ a variety of techniques and objects to help them perform their magic. These can include a magic circle to work within, and robes, crystals, herbs, candles, and various objects to symbolize the four elements. However, none of these are essential. A magician can close his or her eyes and visualize the desired change. Someone who is praying is likely to do exactly the same.

The sample ritual in chapter 11 involves a magic circle. Once you have created your magic space and protected yourself with the four archangels, you can say your prayers or perform magic inside it.

---

61. Charles Jackson, ed., *Yorkshire Diaries and Autobiographies in the Seventeenth and Eighteenth Centuries* (Durham, England: Andrews and Company, 1877), 53.

62. Oliver Heywood, *His Autobiography, Diaries, Anecdote and Event Books, Volume IV,* edited by J. Horsfall Turner (London: Brighouse and Company, 1882. Republished by Whitefish, MT: Kessinger Publishing, 2007), 31–32.

If you are performing magic, you will probably have objects that symbolize the four elements on your altar. A wand or lit candle can symbolize the element of fire, a goblet containing wine or water can symbolize the element of water, a small bell can symbolize earth, and a miniature sword or dagger can symbolize air.

You will also need to wear special clothes while performing your magic. Loose-fitting robes made from natural materials work well, although you can wear any type of clothing, or none at all, if you wish. It is a good idea to change into special clothing when performing magic, as doing so reminds you that you are entering into a special, sacred state. I prefer to work barefooted, as this keeps me grounded.

Before starting, you must have a clear idea about the purpose of your magic. This should be as detailed and precise as possible. For instance, if you are performing magic to generate the necessary money to go on vacation, you will need to know in advance the type of service you'll offer to earn the money. You should know the exact amount of money you will require. You should also know where you plan to have your vacation, and as much as possible about it. You will need much more money if you intend to stay at a five-star resort than you would at a trailer park, for instance. Where will you eat? While you're on vacation, would you like to eat at expensive restaurants or economize and eat at fast-food outlets?

Will you need additional money for entertainment, or other purposes?

Once you have determined exactly what you want, write it down in the form of an affirmation. This means you should write it in the present tense, and avoid any negativity. For instance, you might write, "I am enjoying a wonderful vacation." You would not write, "I will enjoy a wonderful vacation." Similarly, you would not write, "I am spending time away from my miserable home and my loathsome co-workers." Our thoughts are like magnets, and we attract to us whatever it is we focus on. Consequently, you might write, "I am enjoying time away from my home and work to recharge myself, so I can return revitalized and full of energy."

Here is an example of something the person wanting the vacation might write: "I am enjoying a wonderful vacation at a magnificent five-star resort hotel in Maui. I am making the most of every day, enjoying good, nutritious food in excellent restaurants, scuba diving, sailing, swimming, and relaxing in the sun. I'm willing to accept any opportunities that come my way to enhance my wonderful vacation. I am enjoying this time away from home and work in order to relax, de-stress, and make plans for the future. Every day of my vacation is a blessing and gift I give to myself, because I deserve the very best life has to offer."

You are now ready to start performing magic. Place the affirmation you have written, and the four items that symbolize the elements, on your altar. Enjoy a leisurely bath or shower, and change into clean, loose-fitting, comfortable clothes. Perform the first eight steps of the ritual in chapter 11.

Stand in front of your altar and pick up the item that symbolizes the air element. Hold it as high as you can in your right hand. Read your affirmation out loud, putting as much expression into it as possible. Close your eyes, and visualize yourself doing everything that you have written down. Say "thank you" to the universe, and replace the object that symbolizes air on the altar.

Pick up the object that symbolizes fire. Light the candle, if you are using one. Again, hold this object as high as you can and say your affirmation again. Close your eyes, and visualize it exactly the way you want it to be. Say "thank you," and replace the candle, or whatever symbol you chose for fire, on your altar.

Repeat with both the earth and water elements. You have now used the power of all four elements to attract your desire to you. Spread your arms out wide and face east. Close your eyes and visualize your desire again as clearly as you can. Hold this picture for as long as you can. When the visualization starts to fade, say, "I attract this to me now!" With your arms still outstretched, face south, close your eyes, and visualize your desire again. When you can no longer hold the visualization, say, "I attract this to me now!" Repeat this facing west and finally north.

Complete the ritual by performing steps 10, 11, and 12 of the ritual in chapter 11. You should repeat this ritual on a regular basis until your desire becomes a reality. Remember to thank the universe for bringing your desire into being.

You may wonder why the four elements are involved in this ritual. Each element relates to an aspect of you:

> *Air relates to the spiritual aspects of life*
> *Fire relates to the thinking aspects of life*
> *Water relates to the emotional side of life*
> *Earth relates to the physical aspects of life*

Air could be described as the initial inspiration, the start of a new idea. Fire develops it by thinking about it and making plans. Water adds emotion to the thought, and earth brings the idea into physical reality. By including all four elements in the ritual, you are symbolically harnessing the energy, power, and potential that each of them provides. The four elements also show the various stages that energy goes through before it becomes manifest as physical action.

The four elements contain enormous power. In the next chapter we'll discuss something else that has the power to change lives—mandalas. You are likely to find them useful in both meditation and prayer.

fourteen

Praying with Mandalas

When you fix your heart on one point,
then nothing is impossible for you.
—BUDDHA

In the Eastern tradition, mandalas are frequently used for meditation purposes. The word *mandala* comes from the Sanskrit word for "circle." Consequently, mandalas are usually contained inside a circle. In fact, a plain circle is a rudimentary mandala. Most mandalas are more complex than this, of course, and are used to help people enter the desired state of tranquility and peace that helps them to meditate and ultimately achieve a sense of oneness with the universe.

Mandalas are used in many traditions, including Buddhism, Hinduism, Islam, Jainism, Shintoism, and Taoism. Hindu temples are often constructed in the form of a mandala, with doors at the four cardinal directions.

The lotus is considered a sacred plant, not only because it rises from stagnant water and mud and rests, pure and perfect, on the surface of the water, but also because its radiating petals create a perfect mandala. Lotus petals are also used to symbolize the chakras.

Tibetan monks create beautiful sand mandalas known as *dul-tson-kyil-khor* ("mandala of colored powders"). The monks start by consecrating the ground the mandala will be constructed on, and then draw an outline of the mandala in white ink. The mandala is always constructed from the center outward to symbolize how the world was created from a single cell. The mandala itself is made by pouring colored sand through a fine metal funnel. Most mandalas are made from sand that has been dyed white, red, yellow, green, and blue. Gold is also sometimes used.

Sand mandalas usually contain an outer square that encloses two, three, or four circles. The outermost circle is a ring of fire that symbolizes the burning of ignorance. It also keeps the uninitiated out.

Inside this is a circle of diamonds, which symbolizes illumination. Inside this is another ring that symbolizes perception, and an innermost ring of lotus leaves that symbolizes spiritual rebirth. At the center of the mandala is a square, divided into four triangles. Each triangle contains a small circle, and a fifth circle is drawn in the center of the mandala. Each circle contains a symbol of the five divinities.

Creating a sand mandala provides incredible healing energy. The mandala's task is over as soon as it has been completed. Once it is finished, the mandala is destroyed by sweeping all the sand into the center of the circle and placing it in an urn. The sand is poured into a river and ultimately reaches the ocean, where it spreads peace and harmony throughout the world.

Yantras are complex mandalas that symbolize the energies of different deities, and even the universe itself. The word *yantra* comes from two Sanskrit words. *Yam* means "to support," and *trana* means "freedom from bondage." Consequently, a yantra frees and supports. This allows the person meditating to withdraw into himself or herself and gain contact with the divine being within. Yantras are used in Buddhism and Hinduism as pictorial expressions of a prayer.

There are many books available containing pictures of mandalas. You can use these to meditate on, or you may prefer to construct your own.

Creating Your Own Mandalas

Carl Jung (1875–1961), the famous Swiss psychiatrist, created a mandala every morning for many years, and found the exercise revealed what was going on in his mind at the time he drew them. He experimented with his patients and found mandalas helped them heal themselves mentally and emotionally. The mandalas enabled them to release pain and trauma. This is because the images they drew came directly from their souls. Once they were expressed, they lost their effectiveness and could be released. Dr. Jung even built himself a house in the form of a mandala, at Bollingen, overlooking Lake Geneva.

Mandalas are fun to create. All you need is paper and colored pens, pencils, crayons, or markers. You can create mandalas of any shape, but they are usually drawn inside a circle, the traditional symbol of unity, wholeness, and eternity. Consequently, you should start with circular mandalas before experimenting with other shapes. I usually use a plate to act as my template when drawing a circle.

Pause for a few moments after drawing the circle. Take a few deep breaths, and then pick up a pencil and start drawing. There is no need to concentrate on what you are doing, as you want your subconscious mind to guide your hand. Draw spontaneously, changing colors whenever you feel like it. Naturally, you'll have to watch what you are doing, but do this with mild interest, rather than focusing on the work. Your hand will let you know when your mandala is finished.

If you wish, you can examine your mandala as soon as you have completed it. I prefer to put it aside for a few hours, or even a day, before looking at it. You will find it extremely revealing. Sometimes the meaning is obvious. Dark colors and sharp, jagged shapes indicate negativity, pessimism, and possibly depression. Bright cheerful colors indicate a positive, upbeat mood.

It may be hard at times to decipher the symbolism in your mandalas. The shapes and colors you use can all be interpreted. Squares symbolize balance, and circles depict completion. Carl Jung wrote extensively about "squaring the circle." He felt the square symbolized consciousness and the day-to-day world, and the circle represented the subconscious and the spiritual world. Balancing and harmonizing the square and circle make the hidden, subconscious mysteries conscious. A triangle pointing upward indicates humanity's search for the divine. A downward pointing circle shows God reaching down to humanity.

Colors have a variety of symbolic meanings, depending on context. We have discussed these in chapters 11 and 12. Here are some standard interpretations, for the sake of convenience:

Red: enthusiasm, energy, passion, life

Pink: love, nurturing, compassion

Orange: assertive, joyful, persistent

Yellow: lighthearted, carefree, intelligent

Green: healing, soothing, restful

Blue: truth, sincerity, loyalty

Indigo: idealism, justice, calmness

Violet: spirituality, gentleness, inspiration

White: purity, innocence, protection

Brown: hard work, stability

Black: mystery, sophistication

At times the mandala will not reveal much at first glance, and you might need to think about what is going on in your life as you examine it. A pattern will emerge if you draw mandalas every day for a week or two.

You can also draw mandalas to release a particular problem or concern. All you need do is think about your problem while creating the mandala. Examining the mandala later will provide valuable insights into your concern, and frequently will liberate you from whatever it is.

Questioning Your Mandala

An interesting and effective way to gain additional insights from your mandalas is to ask questions. You can ask the questions silently, out loud, or write them down. Sit quietly, in a relaxed state, and wait for the answer to come. The answers usually appear as thoughts, and come from your soul. The first insights you receive are the most important. If you continue waiting, you may gain additional thoughts, but these are more likely to come from your logical left brain, and be less beneficial.

A former student of mine drew a mandala every day for three months to help her get over the breakup of a relationship. Cyndi was devastated when her partner of fourteen years said he no longer loved her and was leaving. Cyndi told me:

Maybe I'd have understood if someone else was involved. But there was no one. Bill told me he wanted to find himself. I didn't play a part in the future he wanted, so the day after he told me, he moved out. I've spoken to him on the phone a few times since, but I haven't seen him, as he hasn't wanted to see me. I was furious to begin with. I thought he'd wasted fourteen years of my life. Then I remembered the mandalas we drew at your spirituality workshop, and so I started to put all my feelings and emotions into drawing mandalas. They were so therapeutic. I'd still be a mess if I hadn't done it. The first ones were so dark and bleak. I got so angry talking to them. I'd ask them questions, and wouldn't like the answers they gave me. The funny thing is, my mandalas started telling me things were getting better before I was aware of it. After a couple of months I noticed the colors were getting more cheerful, not every day but gradually. Everything is good in my life again, but I've kept on drawing mandalas in a book so I can keep track of my progress.

Chakra Mandalas

You can create mandalas for each of your chakras. Focus on a specific chakra, and visualize it whole, healthy, and balanced. Obviously, the main color of these chakra mandalas will be determined by the specific chakra, but you can use as many additional colors as you wish.

If you sense a specific chakra is out of balance, you can lie down and relax for at least five minutes with your chakra mandala resting on it. The chakra will absorb the energy it needs from your mandala.

You can also hang the seven chakra mandalas in a vertical row in a place that you pass frequently. Each time you walk past, your mandalas will strengthen and energize your chakras.

Praying with Your Mandalas

You can create mandalas for any purpose, including prayer. To create a mandala to help you pray, think about your reason for making the prayer before drawing a mandala. I like to do this several hours ahead of time, if possible. Then, when I create my mandala, I am able to clearly focus on my prayer at the same time. Once you have finished creating it, attach it to a wall at a position that is at eye level when you sit down. Sit down in a straight-backed chair in front of the mandala. Place both feet on the floor and move the chair if necessary to ensure the mandala is approximately six feet away from you. Rest your right hand, palm uppermost, in the palm of your left hand on your lap.

Look at your mandala, and take three slow, deep breaths, holding each breath for a few seconds before exhaling. Continue gazing at your mandala, and think of your reason for praying. Blink only when necessary.

When you feel ready, talk to God while continuing to look at your mandala. When you have finished your prayer, continue looking at the mandala for two or three minutes, and be aware of your thoughts. Answers to your concerns might come to you as thoughts at this time. You will probably also receive random thoughts that are not related to your concern. Gently dismiss them, and focus on your mandala again.

The whole process should take about five to seven minutes. Stop whenever you feel the time is right, stand up, stretch, and carry on with your day. You may receive further insights during the day. I usually have a pen and paper with me at all times, and I find it helpful to write down any thoughts or ideas that occur to me during the day.

You can use the same mandala as many times as you wish, as long as your concern does not change. I tend to draw a new mandala each time, as I find that drawing it while thinking of my concern seems to impregnate the mandala with additional spiritual energy. I keep my used mandalas in a folder. It can be helpful and revealing to go through them at a later date, and see what they were telling me, even though I may have failed to recognize it at the time.

You can also pray using mandalas you have chosen from a book. You can infuse your own energy into them by redrawing them, while thinking of your request. Alternatively, you can simply use a mandala that seems right for you at the time.

fifteen

Praying with Angels

For he shall give his angels charge over thee,
to keep thee in all thy ways.

—PSALM 91:11

Angels are supernatural beings of light. The word *angel* comes from the Greek *angelos*, which means "messenger." Not surprisingly, their main task is to transmit messages between humanity and God. In addition, they serve, worship, and attend to God.

According to Jewish tradition, angels were created on the second day of Creation. Unlike humans, who are constantly evolving, angels were perfect from the very beginning, and are constantly aware of their role in sustaining God's creation.

Angels have communicated with people on countless occasions. In the book of Genesis, the "angel of the Lord" appeared to Hagar, a young, pregnant serving girl who was fleeing from Abram's wife, Sarai. The angel told her to return home. He also told her she would give birth to a son who would be called Ishmael (Genesis 16:7–12).

Archangel Gabriel is God's principal messenger. It was Gabriel who told Mary that she'd give birth to the son of God. Tradition says that Gabriel also told the shepherds in the fields about the birth of Jesus, and warned Mary and Joseph to flee to Egypt as Herod's soldiers were searching for the newborn King.

Angels also deliver people's prayers to God. According to Jewish tradition, Metatron, one of the most important angels in heaven, carries prayers through all nine hundred heavens and delivers them to God. Sandalphon, the giant angel who is sometimes referred to as Metatron's twin brother, weaves garlands out of prayers written in Hebrew, and God wears these on His head.

Tradition says that angels are always present when people are praying. Your guardian angel is always with you, anyway. According to Catholic tradition, everyone is assigned a guardian angel when he or she is born. This angel guides and protects the person throughout his or her lifetime, and ultimately helps the person make the transition through death.

Belief in guardian angels is extremely old. In ancient Mesopotamia, guardian angels were thought to be personal gods and were called *massar sulmi*. The tradition of guardian angels became part of the belief systems of the Babylonians and Chaldeans, and this belief ultimately flowed in to Judaism, Christianity, and Islam.

Jesus intimated that children have guardian angels when he said, "Take heed that ye despise not one of these little ones; for I say unto you that in heaven their angels do always behold the face of my Father which is in heaven" (Matthew 18:10).

Hermas, the second-century author of the first Christian "bestseller," *The Shepherd of Hermas*, believed that everyone has both a guardian angel ("angel of righteousness") and a demon ("angel of iniquity"). His book describes his conversations with his guardian angel. St. Basil the Great (c.330–79) wrote, "Among the angels, some are in charge of nations, others are the companions of the faithful . . . It is the teachings of Moses that every believer has an angel to guide him as a teacher and shepherd."[63]

---

63. Basil, *Adversus Eunomium*, 3.1, cited in Jean Daniélou, *The Angels and Their Mission*, translated by David Heimann (Dublin: Four Courts Press, 1957), 68. Originally published in French as *Les Anges et Leur Mission*.

St. Patrick (c.387–461), the patron saint of Ireland, had an extremely close relationship with his guardian angel, Victoricus. One of his prayers seems to indicate that he also enjoyed a special relationship with the entire angelic hierarchy:

> *I arise today:*
> *in the might of the Cherubim;*
> *in obedience of Angels;*
> *in ministration of Archangels.*[64]

Most people are not in regular contact with their guardian angel. In fact, many people have no idea they have a guardian angel. This is because, most of the time, your guardian angel will quietly look after you, and will offer advice only when it is requested. People sometimes ask why our guardian angels do not intervene to prevent us from making mistakes. It would certainly make life easier, but we learn from our mistakes, and our guardian angels give us the lessons we need to learn as we progress through life.

Guardian angels sometimes act directly. Sir Ernest Shackleton (1874–1922), the British explorer, wrote that "one more" accompanied him and his party as they made their weary way back from the South Pole.[65]

---

64. St. Patrick, quoted in Harvey Humann, *The Many Faces of Angels* (Marina del Rey, CA: DeVorss and Company, 1986), 4.

65. Benjamin Walker, *Beyond the Body* (London: Routledge & Kegan Paul, 1974), 127.

The Catholic Church has always had a tradition of praying to angels. St. Ambrose (c.339–97), an early Christian father, wrote, "We should pray to the angels who are given to us as guardians."[66]

Pope Pius XI (1857–1939) prayed to his guardian angel at least twice a day. He claimed that whenever he had to speak with someone who might not accept his ideas, he asked his guardian angel to talk with the other person's guardian angel first. The two angels would always come to an understanding, and this enabled the meeting between the two people to proceed smoothly.[67]

Catholic children are taught to pray to their guardian angel in a special prayer:

> *Angel of God, my guardian dear,*
> *To whom God's love commits me here,*
> *Ever this day, be at my side,*
> *To light and guard, rule and guide. Amen.*

You can also call on any of the other angels, if you wish. They are always willing to help. In the Psalms, David explained why angels are prepared to help us:

> *For he shall give his angels charge over thee,*
> *to keep thee in all thy ways. They shall bear thee*

---

66. Ambrose, quoted in *A Select Library of the Nicene and Post-Nicene Fathers of the Christian Church*, edited by Philip Schaff (Edinburgh: T and T Clark, 1989), vol. 10, *De Vidius*, section 9.

67. Harvey Humann, *The Many Faces of Angels* (Marina del Rey, CA: DeVorss and Company, 1986), 5–6.

up in their hands, lest thou dash thy foot against a stone. Thou shalt tread upon the lion and adder: the young lion and the dragon shalt thou trample under feet. Because he hath set his love upon me, therefore will I deliver him: I will set him on high, because he hath known my name. He shall call upon me, and I will answer him: I will be with him in trouble; I will deliver him, and honor him. (Psalm 91:11–15)

St. Teresa of Avila on Prayer

St. Teresa of Avila (1515–82), a founder of the Discalced Carmelite Order and one of the greatest Christian mystics, wrote in her autobiography about her experiences with angels. She first experienced rapture while reciting a hymn as a prayer. She wrote, "This was the first time that the Lord had granted me this grace of ecstasy, and I heard these words: 'I want you to converse now not with men but with angels.' This absolutely amazed me, for my soul was greatly moved and these words were spoken to me in the depths of the spirit."[68]

St. Teresa wrote three books, including *The Way of Perfection* (1573), a book on prayer that is still considered a classic today. St. Teresa compared

---

68. St. Teresa, *The Life of St. Teresa of Avila by Herself* (translated by J. M. Cohen), (London: Penguin, 1987), 172.

prayer to watering a garden to help it produce beautiful flowers and fruits. There are four stages:

1. *Meditation.* St. Teresa compared this to drawing water from a deep well, as it is a slow and laborious process.

2. *Peace and quiet.* St. Teresa related this to drawing water using a water wheel and buckets. It is faster, easier, and less laborious than drawing water by hand. When the mind and body are quiet, the soul loses interest in earthly concerns, and is open to receive advice and guidance. The soul is, in effect, watered.

3. *Prayer of union.* At this stage, the prayer and God make contact. There are no concerns, stress, or worry, and all the senses are fully occupied with God. At this stage, the garden appears to water itself, possibly from a spring or small stream.

4. *God.* At this stage God takes over, watering the garden with gentle rain. The prayer rests in a state of receptivity and contemplation, and the person enters a type of trance state.

St. Teresa frequently found herself crying tears of joy when she came out of deep prayer.

St. Teresa's most profound experience with an angel occurred in 1559, when an angel pierced her heart with an arrow of love. This incident became known as "the transverberation of St. Teresa." *Transverberation* means "to pierce."

On this occasion, St. Teresa saw a short, beautiful angel with a face that was "so aflame that he appeared to be one of the highest rank of angels, who seem to be all on fire."[69] He was carrying a golden spear, which he plunged into her heart several times. Each time he pulled the spear out, she felt as if he was pulling out her innermost parts, while simultaneously infusing her with an intense love of God.

How to Contact Your Guardian Angel

This is a simple exercise that many people have found helpful to gain angelic awareness and to contact their guardian angel. Make sure you will be undisturbed for approximately thirty minutes. I like to disconnect the phone temporarily to ensure there will be no interruptions.

1. Sit down in a comfortable chair and relax. I sometimes use a recliner chair, but seldom do I attempt an exercise of this sort while lying down, as I usually fall asleep in the middle of the exercise if I do.

2. Take ten slow, deep breaths. Focus on your breathing. Hold each breath for a few sec-

---

69. St. Teresa, *The Life of St. Teresa of Avila by Herself*, 210.

onds, and say to yourself "relax, relax, relax" each time you exhale.

3. Mentally scan your body to make sure you are totally relaxed. Focus on any areas that are still tense, and allow them to relax completely.

4. When you feel totally relaxed, think about your desire to communicate with your guardian angel. Thank your guardian angel for guiding, supporting, and helping you throughout your life. Tell your guardian angel that you'd like to establish a closer connection, and would like to communicate on a regular basis. Ask if this is possible.

5. Wait silently, and see what sort of reply you receive. You may be fortunate, and receive an answer the first time you do this exercise. If so, you can express your love and gratitude, and continue communicating with your guardian angel. Do not feel disappointed if you receive no response on your first several attempts to make contact. You have lived your entire life without making angelic contact, and your guardian angel may be testing you. Your guardian angel will eventually speak with you. It might be in the form of thoughts that suddenly appear in your mind. You will know they are from your guardian angel because the quality and energy of the

messages will be different from your normal thoughts. You might receive messages in the form of dreams, or even receive signs in other ways. Many people, myself included, have experienced seeing white feathers when angels were around.

6. No matter what response you received, and even if you received no response at all, thank your guardian angel for listening to you, and promise to communicate again soon.

7. Take three slow, deep breaths, become familiar with the room around you, and open your eyes.

Writing to Your Guardian Angel

An excellent way to make contact is to write a letter to your guardian angel. You naturally focus your attention on your letter while writing it, which helps facilitate angelic contact. You should write your letter as if writing to a close friend. If you have not already communicated with your guardian angel, you should use your first letters to ask for a closer connection. Once you have made contact, future letters can contain requests for anything you need.

Your letters should also include information on what is going on in your life. Tell your guardian angel about your relationships, family, health, work, hopes, and dreams. Writing all of this down helps clarify any difficulties in your life, and you may find that you see them in a different perspective.

Finish your letter by thanking your guardian angel for looking after you. Express your love and gratitude, and sign your name. Seal the letter inside an envelope and address it to your guardian angel.

You now need to "mail" your letter to your guardian angel. Do this in your sacred space, if you have one. Light a white candle, and sit in front of it with your letter in your cupped hands. Gaze at the flame and think about everything your guardian angel does for you. Express your thanks, and burn the envelope in the candle flame. Watch the smoke send your message up to your guardian angel. Say another quiet "thank you" as the final pieces of the envelope and letter turn into smoke. Carry on with your day, confident that your guardian angel has received your letter.

Naturally, you must be careful whenever you use candles. I place my candles on a metal tray, and I always have water available—just in case of an accident. I have never needed the water, but I find it reassuring to know it's there if necessary.

How to Involve the Angels in Your Prayers

You can include the angels in any prayer. You might, for instance, ask your guardian angel to deliver your prayer for you. If you feel a certain angel has a special interest in the subject you are praying about, you can ask that angel to deliver your prayer.

Become aware of an angelic presence whenever you are praying. This sense of knowing that you are protected and guided by the angelic kingdom will give added strength to your prayers, as well as feelings of comfort and security.

The angels are willing to help you in any way they can. All you need do is ask them.

Nothing could be more important than healing. If you ask them, the angels will be delighted to assist you in your healing prayers. We'll discuss prayers of healing in the next chapter.

sixteen

Healing Prayers

Health is a large word. It embraces not the body only, but the mind and spirit as well . . . and not today's pain or pleasure alone, but the whole being and outlook of a man.
—JAMES H. WEST

Hospitals around the world are full of people who are sick and dying. Not surprisingly, their family and friends often pray that they will recover from their illnesses and regain their health and vitality. People have done this for thousands of years.

As far back as the sixth century BCE, Pythagoras, the Greek philosopher, combined healing and religion in his mystery school. Hippocrates (c.460–c.377 BCE), known as the "father of medicine," was the most famous physician of antiquity. He healed by the laying on of hands. Plato (c.428–347 BCE) cited his teacher, Socrates, when he said, "If the head and body are to be well, you must begin by curing the soul: that is the first thing."[70]

There are many examples in the Bible that demonstrate the healing power of prayer:

> *So Abraham prayed unto God: and God healed Abimelech, and his wife, and his maidservants; and they bore children.* (Genesis 20:17)

> *And Moses cried unto the Lord, saying, Heal her now, O God, I beseech thee.* (Numbers 12:13)

King Hezekiah prayed for healing after his life was threatened with an ulcerous boil. The prayers, plus a poultice of figs, gave the king an additional fifteen years of life (2 Kings 20:1–11).

> *And it came to pass, that the father of Publius lay sick of a fever and of a bloody flux: to whom Paul entered in, and prayed, and laid his hands on him, and healed him.* (Acts 28:8)

> *Is any sick among you? Let him call for the elders of the church; and let them pray over him, anointing him with oil in the name of the Lord.*

---

70. Plato, quoted in Ronald C. Finucane, *Miracles and Pilgrims: Popular Beliefs in Medieval England* (London: J. M. Dent & Sons, 1977), 79.

> *And the prayer of faith shall save the sick, and the Lord shall raise him up; and if he hath committed sins, they shall be forgiven him.* (James 5:14–15)

The Qur'an contains guidance that is intended to promote healing:

> *O mankind! There has come to you a direction from your Lord and a healing for the (diseases) in your hearts—and for those who believe, a Guidance and a Mercy.* (Sura 10:57)

> *We send down (stage by stage) in the Qu'ran that which is a healing and a mercy to those who believe: to the unjust it causes nothing but loss after loss.* (Sura 17:82)

There are many good examples of the healing power of prayer, such as the experience of Myrtle Page Fillmore (1845–1931). Young Myrtle had never enjoyed good health, but she graduated from college and became a schoolteacher. In her twenties she spent a year in the hospital with tuberculosis, a disease that had killed several of her close relatives. Her life improved at the age of thirty-five, when she married Charles Fillmore (1854–1948) and started a family. In 1886 she was told she had just six months to live. She and her husband began searching for a spiritual solution, and attended a series of lectures by E. B.

Weeks, a teacher of Christian Science. Weeks told her that she did not inherit sickness. Myrtle Fillmore changed her entire belief system based on this information. She started praying daily, following a regime of denials and affirmations. She denied the power of her illness and her lifelong belief that she'd inherited the disease. She affirmed radiant health and divine energy radiating into every part of her body. One year later she was completely cured.

She started sharing her experiences with others. Her husband, who had also had health problems, studied the effect of prayer on healing. In 1889 the Fillmores founded Unity, which in 1903 became the Unity School of Christianity, still a thriving organization today.

Affirmative prayer has always been one of the main aspects of Unity, and the Silent Unity prayer ministry receives more than four thousand calls each day from people seeking help. The Silent Unity phone operators have always answered their phones with, "Silent Unity, how may we pray with you?"[71]

Over the last forty years, scientists have been studying the effects of prayer on healing. In 1988 Dr. Randolph Byrd published the results of a study he had conducted five years earlier using cardiac

---

71. Silent Unity can be contacted twenty-four hours a day, seven days a week at 1-800-669-7729. You can also request prayer support at http://unity.org/prayer/index.html (accessed 25 March 2009).

patients in coronary care at a hospital in San Francisco. Three hundred and ninety-three patients who were "statistically inseparable," which means they all had similar symptoms and were in the same general state of health, were randomly split into two groups. One group received intercessory prayer, and the other didn't. The doctors, medical staff, and patients had no idea who was in each group. Each person who was being prayed for was assigned between three and seven Christians from a selection of Protestant churches and the Roman Catholic Church. Each intercessor (person doing the praying) prayed for the person every day, asking for a speedy recovery with no complications.

When the experiment was over, Dr. Byrd found a noticeable difference between the two groups. Almost 85 percent of the people being prayed for rated "good" on the rating system used. This meant they were less likely to have a heart attack, or need antibiotics or other intervention; 73.1 percent of the people who were not prayed for also rated "good." Dr. Byrd published his findings in the *Southern Medical Journal* in July 1988.[72]

---

72. Randolph C. Byrd, "Positive Therapeutic Effects of Intercessory Prayer in a Coronary Care Unit Population." Article in *Southern Medical Journal*, vol. 81, no. 7 (July 1988), 826–29. This article can also be found online at http://www.geocities.com/CapeCanaveral/Lab/6562/apologetics/smj.pdf (accessed 25 March 2009).

Not surprisingly, many other studies followed Dr. Byrd's experiment. Some produced similar results,[73] but others have been unable to demonstrate the efficacy of prayer. However, Dr. David R. Hodge, an assistant professor of social work in the College of Human Services at Arizona State University, analyzed the results of seventeen major studies into intercessory prayer and found that "prayer offered on behalf of another yields positive results."[74] Dr. Hodge's findings are important, as they are a synthesis of seventeen different studies, which effectively eliminates any unconscious biases.

Research is continuing. Since 1995, Harvard Medical School has conducted annual conferences on "Spirituality and Healing in Medicine." In 1999, 48 percent of the medical schools in the United States offered courses in spirituality and health, whereas

---

73. Dr. William S. Harris repeated Dr. Byrd's experiment in Kansas City, Missouri, in 1999; 67.4 percent of his patients who were prayed for scored "good," compared to 64.5 percent of the control group. See William S. Harris, PhD, et al, "A Randomized, Controlled Trial of the Effects of Remote Intercessory Prayer on Outcomes in Patients Admitted to the Coronary Care Unit," *Archives of Internal Medicine*, 25 October 1999, 2273–78. This article can be found online at http://www.ntskeptics.org/issues/prayer/prayer-pap-ioi90043.pdf (accessed 25 March 2009).

74. Dr. David R. Hodge, quoted in Stephen Des Georges, "Does God Answer Prayer? ASU Research Says 'Yes,'" *ASU News*, 23 February 2007. Online at http://asunews.asu.edu/node/1545 (accessed 25 March 2009).

only one-fifth of 1 percent of them offered such courses in 1994.[75]

An intriguing article in *Jet* magazine reported on a study conducted by the Duke University Medical Center in Durham, North Carolina. This study looked at more than four thousand people who were more than sixty-five years old. The researchers discovered that the participants who prayed regularly and attended weekly church services had lower blood pressure than the participants who did neither. In fact, the more the person prayed and attended church, the lower his or her blood pressure was.[76]

Nothing could be more important than healing. You can help people enormously by praying for them when they are unwell. People have always prayed for healing, and it's possible more prayers are made for healing than for anything else. Your prayers can be made even more effective if you tell the people for whom you are praying that you are praying for them.[77]

Obviously, you should ask the divine to help the person you are praying for. You should also ask God

---

75. Jeff Levin, PhD, *God, Faith, and Health* (New York: Wiley, 2001), 9–10.

76. "Can Prayer Lower High Blood Pressure?" Unattributed article in *Jet* magazine, 31 August 1998. This article can be found online at http://findarticles.com/p/articles/mi_m1355/is_n14_v94/ai_21071939 (accessed 18 March 2009).

77. Dr. Arthur Caliandro, *Simple Steps: Ten Things You Can Do to Create an Exceptional Life* (New York: McGraw-Hill, 2000), 155.

to help the sick person gain peace of mind and the necessary inner strength to help him or her handle the illness, and to aid recovery. Also pray for other family members who will be suffering because a loved one is unwell. Pray for the doctors and nurses, and for everyone else who is working to help your sick friend or family member.

Paracelsus (1493–1541), the Swiss alchemist and physician, wrote that "the main reason for healing is love."[78] A medical experiment in 1976 dramatically illustrates this. Ten thousand men suffering from heart disease were surveyed. The men who considered their wives to be supportive and loving experienced a 50 percent reduction in the frequency of chest pain.[79] Most spiritual healers send prayers of love as well as healing, as they realize that both are vital in restoring the person's health.

How to Pray for Healing

Whenever possible, ask the people for whom you are praying to give you permission to include them in your prayers. Obviously, this will not always be

---

78. Paracelsus, quoted in Larry Chang, ed., *Wisdom for the Soul: Five Millennia of Prescriptions for Spiritual Healing* (Washington, DC: Gnosophia Publishers, 2006), 364.

79. H. Medalie and U. Goldbourt, "Angina Pectoris Among 10,000 Men II: Psychosocial and Other Risk Factors as Evidenced by a Multivariate Analysis of Five-Year Incidence Study," *American Journal of Medicine* 60, 1976, 910–21.

possible. If someone is unconscious, or you are unable to contact him or her, you will be unable to request permission first. You might think everyone would welcome a healing prayer, but this is not always the case. Some people have a vested interest in being unwell. It might gain them attention they lacked before. It might make them feel special or important.

Healing prayer is a nine-step process:

1. Sit or lie down comfortably and relax all the muscles in your body.

2. Allow feelings of love for all humanity to build up inside you. Focus on these feelings of love and allow them to penetrate into every part of your body.

3. Say, silently or out loud, a healing prayer. You might create a healing prayer of your own, or find something suitable in a book of prayers. Here is a prayer that you might be able to adapt to suit you and your needs: *Almighty Creator of the Universe, I humbly ask you to send your divine healing energy to all who are sick, suffering, or in pain. Please enfold them with your love, and restore their health and vitality. In particular, I request healing for [name the person or people for whom you are praying]. Thank you. Amen.*

4. Visualize the person you are praying for as clearly as possible. In your mind's eye, see the person you are praying for surrounded by a pure, white healing light. Sense it building up inside your friend until he or she is totally surrounded, internally and externally, with God's healing energy. Hold this image for as long as you can. Ask the divine for healing.

5. Send love to the person you are praying for. In your mind's eye picture him or her receiving your love, and responding to it in a positive way.

6. Visualize the person you are praying for restored to vibrant health. See him or her full of energy, and fit and well again.

7. Thank divine spirit for restoring the health of the person you are praying for. You might say something along the lines of: *Thank you, divine spirit. I pray that all who are in need of your help receive it at this time. May they be filled with your strength, love, and comfort. Thank you for enabling me to request healing for [name the person or people for whom you are praying]. Thank you, God. Thy will be done. Amen.*

8. If you are praying for more than one person, repeat steps 4 to 7.

9. Remain in a state of quiet contemplation for a minute or two. Feel God's divine love restoring your soul and filling you with energy. When you feel ready, open your eyes and carry on with your day.

You can request healing for yourself as well as for others. When you're praying using the nine steps listed above, just insert the word *myself* instead of the name of another person.

It is important to have total faith. There is no need to worry anymore about the person you have prayed for. You have asked God for a healing, and you must have complete faith that Universal Spirit is working on your concern. Repeat the healing prayer every day for as long as necessary.

You should also send healing prayers to enemies and people you don't like. You might be surprised to find how liberating and freeing this is. It will help you to eliminate all the problems, concerns, and negativity from the past.

You might also be surprised to discover that you can send healing to your pets and plants in the same way. Pets and plants both respond extremely well to love. Fill yourself with divine love and allow it to gather in the palms of your hands. Stroke your pets, and notice how they respond to your healing touch. With plants, place your hands on each side of them, and pray for them while sending them your love.

Healing Yourself with Your Guardian Angel

Your guardian angel has your best wishes at heart all the time. He or she will be happy to help you gain relief from any non-life-threatening illness. If, for instance, you are suffering from a tension headache, spend a few minutes communing with your guardian angel. After this, you are likely to find the headache has disappeared. For more serious concerns, lie down and tell your guardian angel about your problem, and allow him or her to lay hands on the afflicted part of your body, sending divine healing energy to you. Obviously, you should combine anything more serious than a tension headache with medical treatment. After all, God might be sending you healing through your medical practitioner.

Raphael, Archangel of Healing

The four main archangels are Raphael, Michael, Gabriel, and Uriel. The name Raphael means "God heals." Raphael has been associated with many examples of divine healing. In the Jewish tradition, Raphael healed Abraham after his circumcision. He also cured Jacob's dislocated hip after he had spent an entire night fighting.[80]

Raphael is probably best known as a healing angel because of the story of Tobias that is recorded

---

80. Louis Ginzberg, *The Legends of the Jews, Volume 1* (Philadelphia: The Jewish Publication Society of America, 1954), 385.

in the Book of Tobit, one of the Apocryphal texts. (This means that it is included in the Roman Catholic Bible but is not in the Protestant Bible.) This story also shows how God answers people's prayers in different ways.

Tobit was a good Jewish man who had been blind for eight years. Because of this, he was unable to make a living and his family had fallen on hard times. Tobit sent a prayer to God asking for death. Tobit's prayer arrived in heaven at the exact same moment as a prayer from a young woman named Sarah. Sarah was possessed by a demon that had killed all seven of her husbands on their wedding nights. She also found life was not worth living. God sent Raphael to answer both prayers.

Tobit began settling his affairs, and asked his son, Tobias, to go to Medina to collect money he was owed. As it was too dangerous to travel on his own, Tobias found a guide to accompany him. This guide was Raphael, but Tobias did not know that.

Tobias and his guide spent the first night of the journey camping beside a river. A large fish tried to swallow Tobias' foot. Tobias caught the fish, which provided them with food. The guide told Tobias to preserve the heart, liver, and gallbladder, as they could be used to make a powerful medicine.

As they neared their destination, the guide told Tobias about Sarah and her problems. He suggested that Tobias marry her and, amazingly, Tobias agreed.

On the wedding night, Tobias burned the heart and liver of the fish on a fire in the bridal chamber. This exorcized the demon, who fled to "the uppermost parts of Egypt." Sarah's father had been so convinced that Tobias would die on the wedding night that he'd already dug a grave for him. He was delighted to see the couple come out of the room the next morning, and gave Tobias half his fortune. The family returned home, and the guide told Tobias to rub the fish's gallbladder on his father's eyes. This restored his eyesight.

Tobit and Tobias were so grateful that they offered half of their fortune to the guide. He turned it down, saying, "I am Raphael, one of the seven holy angels, which present the prayers of the saints, and go in before the glory of the Holy One . . . Be not afraid, ye shall have peace; but bless God for ever. For not any favor of mine, but by the will of your God I came; wherefore bless Him for ever."[81] Now that he had answered the prayers of both Tobit and Sarah, Raphael returned to heaven.

This story was a favorite of Renaissance artists, who loved depicting Raphael and Tobias, usually with a fish.

---

81. *The Apocrypha: Translated out of the Greek and Latin Tongues Being the Version Set Forth* AD *1611 Compared with the Most Ancient Authorities and Revised* AD *1894* (London: Folio Society, 2006), 84. (Originally published jointly by Oxford University Press and Cambridge University Press, 1895.)

Because Archangel Raphael is so interested in healing, you can ask him for help in healing yourself and others.

You can also call on Archangel Michael, as he is also considered a healing angel. An old Christian tradition says that Michael created a healing spring at Chairotopa, near Colossae in what is now Turkey. People who bathed in it and invoked the Blessed Trinity and Michael were said to be healed of their illnesses. Michael caused another healing spring to come from a rock at Colossae. The local pagans tried to destroy it by directing a stream to cross its path. Michael split the rock with a lightning bolt, creating a new path for the stream and ensuring his healing spring remained forever. In addition to this, Michael banished a pestilence that was killing the people in Rome at the time of St. Gregory the Great.

Praying with Others for Healing

Prayers become even more effective when performed with others. This is one reason why people go to churches, temples, and synagogues. If you are praying for someone in a group situation, you should appoint someone to say the prayers out loud. I find it helpful to write the prayers with the other people who will be praying beforehand. The act of writing the prayers is a form of praying in itself.

If you are praying for healing for a large number of people, you should write their names in a healing book, and ask the divine to heal everyone who is listed in the book. Many churches do this.

Praying for People Who Are Dying

Obviously, this is a sad situation for everyone concerned. If the person is dying, you should pray to God asking for a merciful and peaceful end to his or her suffering. It might seem cruel or unfair, especially when a young person dies, and you are likely to have mixed emotions. In the case of an illness, you may feel your prayers for healing have not been answered. This is no reason to stop praying. Continue praying for the best interests of the person who is dying, and continue to pray for this person after he or she has passed over. Thank God for enabling this person to be in your life, and rejoice in the life he or she has had.

Unanswered Healing Prayers

Unfortunately, healing prayer does not always work. This can be devastating, especially when loved ones die despite our best efforts. No one knows why healing prayers can sometimes cause a miracle to occur, but at other times seem to do nothing at all. There is no point in blaming the patient or the person doing the praying.

Unfortunately, I have met several people who temporarily lost their faith because their healing prayers had not been answered. It is important to remember that even when our prayers appear to be unanswered, we still need to pray that the divine's will be done.

I also know people who are skeptical about the benefits of praying for people who request healing. This skepticism may have been caused by the exposure of fake faith healers on television,[82] or by personal experiences of unanswered prayer. A certain amount of skepticism can be a good thing, as long as it is honest skepticism rather than a closed mind.

St. Augustine (354–430) was originally skeptical about the power of healing prayer, and wrote in his early works that Christians should not expect the healing gift of Jesus to continue. However, in the year 424 an incident occurred that totally changed his mind. A brother and a sister both suffered from convulsions. They started coming to Augustine's church every day and prayed for healing. On the second Sunday before Easter, after they had been praying for many weeks, the young man was in the crowded church praying as usual. Suddenly he collapsed, and the people close to him moved away quickly, as they thought he had died. However, after a few moments,

---

82. James Randi, *The Faith Healers* (Buffalo, NY: Prometheus Books, 1987).

the young man stood up, completely cured. Augustine was so amazed that he invited the young man to his home for dinner to discuss exactly what had happened.

On the third day after Easter, Augustine asked the brother and sister to stand in full view of the congregation while he read a letter he had received from the young man. Everyone could see the man was standing normally, but the woman was still trembling and convulsing. After reading the letter, Augustine began a sermon on healing, but was quickly interrupted by shouts from his audience. The young woman had fallen to the ground. She quickly stood up, and everyone could see that she was healed. Augustine wrote, "Praise to God was shouted so loud that my ears could scarcely stand the din."[83]

Obviously this is an exceptional example, but miracles are still occurring every day.

In the next chapter we'll look at the rosary and other methods of prayer that can be used for general, as well as healing, purposes.

---

83. St. Augustine, *The City of God* (translated by Gerald G. Walsh and Daniel J. Honan), (New York: Fathers of the Church, 1954), 450.

seventeen

Additional Methods to Enhance Your Prayers

God warms his hands at man's heart when he prays.
—JOHN MASEFIELD

A s you have seen, there are many different ways to pray. This chapter describes techniques and objects that many people have found helpful while saying their prayers.

The Novena

The novena is a repetitive prayer that is particularly popular in the Catholic tradition. However, it is also becoming increasingly popular with people of different faiths and denominations. The word *novena* comes from the Latin word *novem*, which means "nine." Consequently, a novena prayer is repeated every day for nine consecutive days.

Catholics believe that the novena prayer dates back to the nine days Mary and the disciples spent praying together between Ascension and Pentecost Sunday. On the ninth day, the Holy Spirit descended on them from heaven as tongues of fire (Acts 1, Acts 2:1–4).

However, the novena prayer predates this. The ancient Greeks and Romans prayed for their dead friends and relatives for nine days after the person died. A feast was held on the ninth day to conclude the funeral rites. Roman families also celebrated an annual *parentalia novendialia* (February 13 to 22), which commemorated all the deceased members of a family. Again, a feast was held on the ninth day. There are four main types of novenas:

1. Novenas of mourning after someone has died. The *novemdiales*, the nine days following the death of a pope, is a good example.

2. Novenas of preparation. These include the nine days before Easter and Christmas.

3. Novenas of prayer. These are prayers offered to the saints and angels, and also to Mary and

Jesus. There is always a particular intention behind these prayers.

4. Indulgenced novenas. These are novenas made to "purchase" God's forgiveness for a sin the person has committed.

In the Catholic tradition a particular saint or angel is prayed to for nine days. Mary and Jesus are also frequently prayed to in novena prayer. The exact person or angel to pray to is determined by the nature of the prayer. Marital problems, for instance, can be resolved by praying the novena to St. Rita of Cascia, as she had a particularly difficult marriage. Infertility can be overcome by praying to St. Anne, who was married twenty years before giving birth to the mother of Jesus. Healing prayers should be made to St. Raphael. The most popular saints for novena prayers are St. Anthony of Padua (overcoming debt, finding lost items, and helping the poor), St. Rita of Cascia (marital difficulties and impossible situations), and St. Jude (helping people in difficult or hopeless situations, and achieving the impossible).

There are formal prayers for every type of situation. Repeating your prayers for nine consecutive days is a powerful way to pray, as each repetition adds force to the prayer. You do not need an intermediary, unless you specifically desire one. In my experience, a good way to perform a novena prayer is to both write and pray the prayer on the first day. Keep the prayer on your altar for the full nine days, and repeat it every day along with your other prayers.

Prayer Beads

More than two-thirds of the religious people in the world use prayer beads in their religious practices.[84] Although prayer beads have a variety of forms, their aim is usually the same: to help people recite and count their prayers and incantations. Beads have been related to prayer for thousands of years. The word *bead* comes from the Anglo-Saxon word *bede*, which means "prayer."

In the West, the best-known prayer beads are rosaries. These are usually associated with prayers in the Roman Catholic and Greek Orthodox traditions. Buddhist monks also keep track of their sutras with prayer beads. However, it is not uncommon today for Pagans and people of other religions to use prayer beads to help them pray and meditate.

Prayer beads are thought to have originated in India almost three thousand years ago. Hindu mystics used 108 identical beads, made from the seeds of sacred plants, to help focus their attention while

---

84. Hillary Katch and Mary French, "Prayer Beads: A Cultural Experience." Exhibit at the University of Missouri Museum of Anthropology in Columbia, MO, Winter 2004. Summary online at http://anthromuseum.missouri.edu/minigalleries/prayerbeads/intro.shtml (accessed 25 March 2009).

chanting sacred words. Buddhists were quick to adopt the practice. Christianity and Islam adopted the rosary, too, but changed the number of beads to suit their requirements. The oldest Christian rosary has 150 beads, symbolizing the 150 psalms.

Christian Rosaries

Eastern Christian monks began using prayer beads in the third century.[85] St. Benedict of Nursia (c.480–c.547) wanted his disciples to pray all 150 psalms at least once every week. Because this was an almost impossible task to do from memory, 150 *Pater Nosters* were said instead. (This is the Lord's Prayer. *Pater Noster* is Latin for "Our Father.") Because of this, rosaries of 150 beads were called *paternosters*.

The famous, or perhaps infamous, Lady Godiva (c.997–1067) bequeathed her set of paternoster beads to the convent she founded in 1057. This gives her another claim to fame, as it is the first recorded mention of Christian prayer beads. Benedictine monks still use the paternoster rosary today. Despite this early interest in the rosary, the Roman Catholic Church did not officially accept prayer beads until 1520, when Pope Leo X gave them his approbation.

Nowadays, most Catholics use the Marian rosary, which contains fifty-nine beads. This dates

---

85. *Encyclopaedia Britannica, Micropaedia VIII*, 15th edition (Chicago: Encyclopaedia Britannica, 1974), 670.

back to St. Dominic (1170–1221), who created them after seeing a vision of the Virgin Mary and three angels while praying for three days and nights in a forest near Toulouse. Another version of this story says he was praying in a *rosarium* (rose garden). This version might have been an attempt to explain why prayer beads are known as *rosaries*. At one time, beads made from crushed rose petals were used in rosaries. As the Virgin Mary has always been symbolized by a rose, and the rosary is used in Marian prayers, it is more likely the name came from this.

Most prayer beads in the Hindu, Buddhist, Christian, and Islamic traditions contain a set number of identical beads, with possibly one or two different-sized beads to aid counting or to serve a specific role in the person's prayers. Pagan prayer beads are quite different, as they employ a large variety of beads of different colors, shapes, and sizes.

As well as helping people to keep track of their prayers, rosaries also symbolize the owner's commitment to prayer, and their circular shape symbolizes unity, perfection, and enlightenment.

Rosaries in the Catholic Tradition

Catholics use the rosary to help them say the required number of "Hail Mary" and "Our Father" prayers, while meditating upon the fifteen mysteries of the

life, death, and resurrection of Jesus.[86] The beads
are made from groups of ten smaller beads and one
larger bead. These are called "decades." The Lord's
Prayer is said on the larger bead, and the Hail Mary
prayer is said on the smaller ones.

The Hail Mary, or Ave Maria, is the most famous
of the prayers addressed to the Virgin Mary. It com-
bines the greeting of Archangel Gabriel to Mary
(Luke 1:28) and Elizabeth's greeting to Mary at the
Visitation (Luke 1:42). The additional words, the
final sentence starting with "Holy Mary, Mother of
God," was added in the Middle Ages. The complete
prayer is:

> *Hail Mary, full of grace, the Lord is with you.*
> *Blessed are you among women,*
> *And blessed is the fruit of your womb, Jesus.*

---

86.   The mysteries of the life, death, and resurrection of Jesus are
known as the Joyful, Sorrowful, and Glorious Mysteries. The first
Joyful Mystery is the Annunciation (Luke 1:28). The second Joyful
Mystery is the Visitation (Luke 1:41–42). The third Joyful Mystery
is the Birth of Jesus (Luke 2:7). The fourth Joyful Mystery is the
Presentation (Luke 2: 22–23). The fifth Joyful Mystery is Finding
the Child Jesus in the Temple (Luke 2:46). The first Sorrowful
Mystery is the Agony in the Garden (Luke 22:44–45). The second
Sorrowful Mystery is the Scourging at the Pillar (John 19:1). The
third Sorrowful Mystery is the Crowning with Thorns (Matthew
27: 28–29). The fourth Sorrowful Mystery is the Carrying of the
Cross (John 19:17). The fifth Sorrowful Mystery is the Crucifixion.
The first Glorious Mystery is the Resurrection (Mark 16:6). The
second Glorious Mystery is the Ascension (Mark 16:19). The third
Glorious Mystery is the Descent of the Holy Ghost (Acts 2:4). The
fourth Glorious Mystery is the Assumption (Revelation 12:1). The
fifth Glorious Mystery is the Coronation (Judith 15: 10–11).

> *Holy Mary, Mother of God, pray for us sinners,*
> *Now and at the hour of our death. Amen.*

In addition to the fifty-four beads in the main circle, the Catholic rosary also has a group of five beads and a crucifix that is outside the circle of five decades. When someone says the rosary, he or she makes a sign of the cross and says the Apostle's Creed while holding the crucifix. He or she says the Lord's Prayer on the first bead, the Hail Mary on each of the next three beads, and "Glory Be to the Father" on the next bead.[87] On the final bead, he or she meditates on the First Mystery, and then starts to work his or her way around the circle of beads.

Rosary novenas combine the rosary with novena prayers to create a nine-day cycle of prayers. There are also fifty-four-day rosary novenas, which were introduced in 1884 after an apparition of the Virgin Mary was seen in Pompeii. This version of the novena requires people to pray five decades of the rosary every day for twenty-seven days in petition, followed by another twenty-seven days in which five decades of the rosary are said every day in thanksgiving.

On October 7 each year, the Roman Catholic Church celebrates the Feast of Our Lady of the

---

87. "Glory be to the Father, and to the Son, and to the Holy Ghost. As it was in the beginning, is now, and ever shall be, world without end. Amen."

Rosary. This date was chosen because Christian soldiers defeated the Turks at the Battle of Lepanto on October 7, 1571. This victory was especially important, as the Christian army had been defeated twice before at this location. On the day of the battle, processions were held in Rome, and the success was attributed to Our Lady of the Rosary. As a result of this, Pope Pius V authorized that the rosary should be commemorated on that day every year.

Hindu Prayer Beads

It is generally believed that prayer beads originated in ancient India. Sandstone carvings dating back to 185 BCE that depict people holding prayer beads have been preserved.[88] As are Buddhist prayer beads, Hindu prayer beads are called *mala*, and are worn around the neck. They contain 108 beads that are used when counting mantras. The number 108 comes from the twelve astrological signs multiplied by the nine planets. Another Hindu mala, the *akshamala*, has fifty beads, which corresponds with the number of letters in the Sanskrit alphabet.

---

88. Eleanor Wiley and Maggie Oman Shannon, *A String and a Prayer: How to Make and Use Prayer Beads* (York Beach, ME: Red Wheel/Weiser, 2002), 5.

Buddhist Prayer Beads

Buddhism began in the fifth century BCE. Prayer beads were introduced almost immediately, and were used for counting breaths and repeating mantras. Buddhist malas usually consist of 108 beads. This probably comes from the Hindu malas, but it is said that 108 Brahmins were present at the birth of Buddha. The circle of beads symbolizes the Wheel of Life and Time. The Buddhists also have malas consisting of fifty-four and twenty-seven beads. Twenty-seven-bead malas are worn around the wrist, and are used because the larger malas would touch the ground during prostrations.

Muslim Prayer Beads

It is not known when Muslims started using prayer beads. However, it is likely to have come from Buddhism. Muslim prayer beads are called *misbaha* or *subha*, from the Arabic verb "to praise." Muslims use strings of ninety-nine beads, with a larger bead that signifies the divine name known only to Allah. The ninety-nine beads represent the different names Allah is referred to in the Qur'an. The beads help Muslims to recite the ninety-nine names, remind them of the litanies, and help them remember and repeat important prayers. The beads create a symbolic chain that connects human beings to the divine.

Pagan Prayer Beads

Interest in prayer beads has increased dramatically among the various Pagan groups. Wiccans create prayer beads to celebrate the eight sabbats, the Triple Goddess, the thirteen lunar months of the year, and the twenty-eight days in a lunar month. Druids create prayer beads to celebrate the Three Worlds. Shamans create prayer beads to commemorate and remember their ancestors. Memorial prayer beads are made to commemorate the deaths of friends or family members.

Prayer beads are also made to commemorate joyful events, such as births, engagements, and weddings. Pagans sometimes present these beads to both the bride and groom to commemorate their vows, and to ensure a long and happy marriage.

Prayer beads can be created for people to carry when they are away from home. This ensures their loved ones remain close, no matter how far they travel.

Beads are also created for individual deities. Most Pagans work with a few selected deities, and prayer beads dedicated to them are often kept on an altar or carried with the person. If someone works with, say, three deities, he or she would have three sets of prayer beads, one for each deity.

Prayer beads can be made for spellcasting or any other magical purpose, and used as a valuable working tool.

Obtaining Your Own Prayer Beads

If you belong to a Christian faith, you might choose to buy a rosary that has been prayed over and blessed by a priest. Rosaries vary enormously in price, depending on the quality of the beads. Other factors also affect their value. Rosaries from the Holy Land are especially prized, as are rosaries that have been in contact with a sacred relic or have been blessed by the Pope. Rosaries from Marian shrines—such as Fatima in Portugal, Knock in Ireland, and Medjugorje in Bosnia and Herzegovina—are also prized. You might find someone in your area who makes rosaries and prayer beads, and be able to buy something suitable from him or her. Alternatively, you may choose to make your own rosary.

Decide on the purpose of your rosary in advance. This means that when you visit a bead store, the beads you require will be easy to find. In fact, in a sense, they will find you. If possible, construct your rosary in a sacred space, and think of your intention in making it whenever you are working on it. When it is finished, consecrate it inside your magic circle or other sacred space. You can now use it in your prayers, meditations, and magical work.

Praying the Scriptures

I recently attended the funeral of a close friend. He was a Christian, and three people, including the minister, read passages from the Bible. They all read their passages well, but one man had me listening intently to every single word he read. I realized afterward that the other two people read their passages, but the third person prayed it. The difference was immense, and several people commented to me afterward on the quality of his reading. It reminded me of the words of William Law (1686–1761), the English clergyman and author, who wrote, "Therefore, the Scriptures should only be read in an attitude of prayer, trusting to the inward working of the Holy Spirit to make their truths a living reality within us."[89]

Listening to this man reading from the Bible made me realize that reading spiritual books, silently or out loud, can be an act of prayer. However, the words must be read rather than skimmed over. You are not reading a popular novel, but a holy book. I find it helpful to scan the words first and then read them again slowly, paying attention to every word. Read for understanding and insight, too. It can be helpful, if you have not done this before, to start by reading familiar passages. Someone from a Christian background might start with the Twenty-third Psalm or the Sermon on the Mount, for instance.

---

89. William Law, *The Power of the Sun*. Originally published in 1761 as *An Humble, Earnest, and Affectionate Address to the Clergy*. Many editions are available; my copy was published by Church Crusade (London, 1923).

Once you have finished reading, pause and think about what you have read. Ask yourself if you can feel in your heart the message you have just read. You may find it helpful to follow your reading with your everyday prayers.

While working on this book, I learned that reading the scriptures this way is known as "holy reading" or "the Benedictine Way."[90]

Another version of this is to select a brief passage from a spiritual text and read it several times. If any phrase or sentence stands out, pay special attention to it. There is no need to analyze the words. Simply focus on it for as long as you can, and then start reading again. Whenever you feel like it, close your eyes and pray.

Another possibility is to read a religious story and then close your eyes and imagine the events you have just read unfolding in your mind. See, hear, smell, and taste everything you can to make the event as real as possible. Feel the emotions the participants in the event must have experienced. If you wish, you can become a participant in the scene. Speak to the other people involved. Ask questions and listen to the answers. Remember that you're a minor participant in the scene, someone who was fortunate enough to witness it, rather than the lead-

---

90. Trevor Hudson, *Invitations to Abundant Life* (Cape Town, South Africa: Struik Christian Books, 1998), 42.

ing character. Once you have experienced the event for as long as you wish, allow the scene to fade and start praying.

Affirmations

Affirmations are thoughts that are constantly repeated to create change in a person. They are always said in the first person and in the present tense. You can repeat them whenever you have a spare moment. To get the maximum benefit from them, it is a good idea to say them in different ways. You can do this by saying them both silently and out loud. You can repeat an affirmation several times, placing the emphasis on a different word each time. You can sing your affirmations. You can whisper them, shout them, or do something in between. You can even write them down. If you do this, sign your name to them. Here are examples of spiritual affirmations that are, in effect, prayer:

I can do all things through Christ which strengtheneth me. (Philippians 4:13)

In him I live, and move, and have my being. (adapted from Acts 17:28)

God is love. (1 John 4:8)

Be still and know that I am God. (Psalm 46:10)

Jesus Christ, have mercy on me, a sinner.
(The Jesus prayer)

I am an important, integral part of the divine plan.

I am a channel for divine energy.

The divine spirit within me brings me peace of mind, radiant health, love, and happiness.

The divine works through me.

I deserve all the good things life has to offer.

I am at peace.

I trust my intuition.

I am God's creation.

I feel the presence of a higher power.

My mind is at peace.

You can say your affirmations whenever you have a spare moment during the day. Instead of getting annoyed at small delays, you'll be able to fill the time profitably with affirmations and prayers that will increase your faith and self-esteem.

Prayer Stones

I was taught this interesting method by a young man in Frankfurt, Germany. While we were enjoying a cup of coffee together, he accidentally dropped a small, round pebble he'd been fiddling with. The coffee shop was busy, and it took him a couple of minutes to find the pebble. I asked him why he'd spent so long trying to find something that seemed worthless.

He explained that it was his prayer stone, and he carried it to help him remain in contact with nature everywhere he went. It also reminded him to pray whenever he felt the smooth stone in his pocket.

The concept of a prayer stone is very old. Muslims consider a stone that is part of the Kaaba in Mecca to be the cornerstone of the earth, and all Muslims around the world intend to make a pilgrimage to see it at least once in their lives.

In the Jewish tradition, visitors to cemeteries place a stone on the grave of a loved one in order to honor the dead. Stone cairns are frequently found at places of pilgrimage where each new pilgrim has added a stone. These cairns ultimately become sacred places in their own right.

Interestingly, if you would like to use this method of prayer, the stone will find you. Keep alert everywhere you go, and sooner or later you will find a small stone that seems to call out to you. Look after it, pray with it, and before long the stone will develop a spiritual awareness that you will be able to sense whenever you touch it.

eighteen

Conclusion

Deep peace of the running waves to you
Deep peace of the flowing air
Deep peace of the smiling stars to you
Deep peace of the quiet earth.
—IRISH BLESSING

I hope you have found this book informative and useful. I also hope it has helped you establish a closer, more intimate connection with the divine.

If you are still hesitating to pray, remember that it is impossible to pray incorrectly. Many people hold back because they are worried they might somehow pray in the wrong way. You cannot get it wrong. Almost two thousand years ago, St. Paul wrote:

> *Likewise the Spirit also helpeth our infirmities: for we know not what we should pray for as we ought: but the Spirit itself maketh intercession for us with groanings which cannot be uttered.* (Romans 8:26)

I love the phrase *groanings which cannot be uttered.* This means that Spirit intercedes with us with signs that are too deep for words. In this passage, St. Paul is saying that we all hesitate to pray, because we're worried that we will make mistakes and get it wrong.

You won't get it wrong. In this book we've covered a variety of different ways to pray, as well as suggestions on how to utilize prayer in your life. Choose a method that appeals to you and experiment with it. Try some of the other methods, too. Be persistent. Nothing worthwhile happens without effort. Remember that you are part of God. Because of this, there are no limits on what you can achieve. Whenever you want divine guidance, it is available.

My wife and I regularly meet another couple, good friends of ours, for dinner. Sometimes we meet at a restaurant, and at other times meet at each other's homes. About two years ago we happened to be in a restaurant, and our friends asked if we'd mind if they said grace before the meal. We were happy to pray with them. Ever since then, we've always said grace each time we've had dinner together. We didn't comment on it the first few times, but finally curiosity got the better of me, and I asked Don about it. He was slightly embarrassed to tell me that his seven-year-old granddaughter had insisted on saying grace when she'd came to stay with them.

"We wanted to encourage her," Don told me. "So we used to say grace whenever she visited. Gradually we started to say it before every meal. We like it. It encourages us to think about God, and gives us a chance to offer thanks for all the blessings in our lives. It actually makes mealtimes much more pleasant, as we're focused on the important aspects of life before we even start to eat. I'm praying much more at other times, too, now. It's changed our lives so much."

Prayer should be a normal part of everyday life. Saying grace before meals is an excellent way for families to pray together. Every member of the family should be encouraged to participate, rather than having the same person say the prayers every time.

You can pray anywhere, at any time. A friend of mine who lived in Korea told me that Christians in Korea say a silent prayer whenever they enter the home of a friend, praying for the home and the people who live in it. The Koreans bow their heads and close their eyes to do this, but that is not necessary. You could help a large number of people if you introduced this practice into your life.

An acquaintance of mine found a box full of old photographs. On an impulse, he prayed for all the people in the photos. He told me that he experienced an incredible feeling of joy after praying for everyone in a class photograph that included him and was taken when he was seven years old.

Pray on your own, with friends, and in religious services. Pray for yourself, for family and friends, for enemies, for people you happen to pass in the street, and for all humanity.

Love yourself, and everyone else. Everyone is part of God. Your love and compassion can bring light into other people's lives, helping them to realize their own divine nature.

Forgive yourself and others. Remember that everyone is doing the best they can at any given moment. You hold yourself back by hanging on to old grudges and perceived hurts.

Express gratitude to the divine every day for the precious gift of life, and for all the other blessings in your life that have come as a direct result of this. Give thanks for the small joys as well as the large. Some of my most precious memories concern seemingly unimportant moments, such as enjoying a cup of coffee with a friend or watching my grandson play a game of soccer. Thanksgiving is an important part of prayer.

Communicate with the divine in your prayers and your thoughts. The rewards are immeasurable.

suggested reading

The Holy Bible. Many editions available. The biblical quotes in this book are from the King James Version, first published in 1611.

The Qur'an. Many editions available. Mine is translated by Abdullah Yusuf Ali. Elmhurst, NY: Tahrike Tarsile Qur'an, Inc., 2001.

Beak, Sera. *The Red Book: A Deliciously Unorthodox Approach to Igniting Your Divine Spark.* San Francisco: Jossey-Bass, 2006.

Berg, Wendy, and Mike Harris. *Polarity Magic: The Secret History of Western Religion.* St. Paul, MN: Llewellyn, 2003.

Blau, Tatjana, and Mirabai Blau. *Buddhist Symbols.* New York: Sterling Publishing, 2003.

Bowker, John. *God: A Brief History.* London: Dorling Kindersley, 2002.

———. *World Religions: The Great Faiths Explored and Explained.* London: Dorling Kindersley, 1997.

Bullen, Anthony F. *The Rosary in Close-Up.* London: Geoffrey Chapman Ltd., 1962.

Butterworth, Eric. *Discover the Power Within You: A Guide to the Unexplored Depths Within.* San Francisco: HarperSanFrancisco, 1992.

de Montfort, St. Louis. *The Secret of the Rosary.* New York: Christ and Country Books, 1965.

Dispenza, Joseph. *God on Your Own: Finding a Spiritual Path Outside Religion.* San Francisco: Jossey-Bass, 2006.

Don, Megan. *Falling into the Arms of God: Meditations with Teresa of Avila.* Novato, CA: New World Library, 2005.

Dossey, Larry. *Be Careful What You Pray For . . . You Just Might Get It.* San Francisco: HarperSanFrancisco, 1997.

———. *Healing Words.* San Francisco: HarperSanFrancisco, 1993.

Doyle, Mary K. *The Rosary Prayer by Prayer*. Geneva, IL: 3E Press, 2006.

Duncan, Anthony. *The Christ, Psychotherapy and Magic*. London: Allen & Unwin, 1969.

Farber, Don. *Tibetan Buddhist Life*. London: Dorling Kindersley, 2003.

Finley, Guy. *The Lost Secrets of Prayer*. St. Paul, MN: Llewellyn, 1998.

Gaulden, Albert Clayton. *Signs and Wonders: Understanding the Language of God*. New York: Atria Books, 2003.

Greer, John Michael, and Clare Vaughn. *Pagan Prayer Beads*. San Francisco: Red Wheel/Weiser, 2007.

Hanh, Thich Nhat. *The Energy of Prayer: How to Deepen Your Spiritual Practice*. Berkeley, CA: Parallax Press, 2006.

Happold, F. C. *Mysticism: A Study and an Anthology*. London: Penguin, 1963. Revised edition 1970.

Heiler, Friedrich (translated by Samuel McComb). *Prayer: A Study in the History and Psychology of Religion*. London: Oxford University Press, 1932.

Hubbard, David A. *The Problem with Prayer Is . . .* Wheaton, IL: Tyndale House Publishers, 1972.

Katra, Jane, and Russell Targ. *The Heart of the Mind: How to Experience God Without Belief*. Novato, CA: New World Library, 1999.

Long, Max Freedom. *The Secret Science at Work: New Light on Prayer*. Los Angeles: Huna Research Publications, 1953.

———. *The Secret Science Behind Miracles*. Los Angeles: Kosmon Press, 1948.

Merton, Thomas. *Contemplation in a World of Action*. London: George Allen & Unwin, 1971.

———. *Contemplative Prayer*. New York: Doubleday, 1990. First published in 1968 as *The Climate of Monastic Prayer* (Kalamazoo, MI: Cistercian Publications).

Noss, John B. *Man's Religions*. New York: Macmillan, 1949. Fifth edition 1974.

Roberts, Elizabeth, and Elias Amidon. *Prayers for a Thousand Years*. San Francisco: HarperSanFrancisco, 1999.

Ryan, Marah Ellis. *Pagan Prayers, Collected by Marah Ellis Ryan*. Chicago: A. C. McClurg & Co., 1913.

Salwak, Dale, ed. *The Power of Prayer*. Novato, CA: New World Library, 1998.

Serith, Ceisiwr. *A Book of Pagan Prayer*. San Francisco: Red Wheel/Weiser, 2002.

Smart, Ninian, and Richard D Hecht, eds. *Sacred Texts of the World*. London: Quercus Publishing, 2007. (Originally published by London: Macmillan and Company, 1982)

Stein, Inez D. *The Magic of Zen*. Atlanta: Humanics Trade, 1996.

Thomas, Keith. *Religion and the Decline of Magic.* New York: Charles Scribner's Sons, 1971.

Walsh, Roger. *Essential Spirituality: The 7 Central Practices to Awaken Heart and Mind.* New York: Wiley, 1999.

Weatherhead, Leslie D. *Psychology in the Service of the Soul.* London: The Epworth Press, 1929.

Webster, Richard. *Color Magic for Beginners.* Woodbury, MN: Llewellyn, 2006.

———. *Gabriel: Communicating with the Archangel for Inspiration & Reconciliation.* St. Paul, MN: Llewellyn, 2005.

———. *Michael: Communicating with the Archangel for Guidance & Protection.* St. Paul, MN: Llewellyn, 2004.

———. *Praying with Angels.* Woodbury, MN: Llewellyn, 2007.

———. *Raphael: Communicating with the Archangel for Healing & Creativity.* St. Paul, MN: Llewellyn, 2005.

———. *Spirit Guides & Angel Guardians.* St. Paul, MN: Llewellyn, 1997.

———. *Talisman Magic: Yantra Squares for Tantric Divination.* St. Paul, MN: Llewellyn, 1995.

———. *Uriel: Communicating with the Archangel for Transformation & Tranquility.* Woodbury, MN: Llewellyn, 2005.

Wiley, Eleanor, and Maggie Oman Shannon. *A String and a Prayer: How to Make and Use Prayer Beads.* York Beach, ME: Red Wheel/Weiser, 2002.

Zaleski, Philip, and Carol Zaleski. *Prayer: A History.* Boston: Houghton Mifflin, 2005.

index